Lodge Hill Camp, Caerleon, and the Hillforts of Gwent

Joshua Pollard, Ray Howell,
Adrian Chadwick and Anne Leaver

with contributions by

Michael Hamilton, Philip Macdonald, Lesley McFadyen,
Elaine Morris, Rick Peterson, Neil Phillips, Ruth Young,
Tim Young and Daryl Williams

BAR British Series 407
2006

Published in 2016 by
BAR Publishing, Oxford

BAR British Series 407

Lodge Hill Camp, Caerleon and the Hillforts of Gwent

ISBN 978 1 84171 935 1

© the authors individually and the Publisher 2006

The authors' moral rights under the 1988 UK Copyright,
Designs and Patents Act are hereby expressly asserted.

All rights reserved. No part of this work may be copied, reproduced, stored,
sold, distributed, scanned, saved in any form of digital format or transmitted
in any form digitally, without the written permission of the Publisher.

BAR Publishing is the trading name of British Archaeological Reports (Oxford) Ltd.
British Archaeological Reports was first incorporated in 1974 to publish the BAR
Series, International and British. In 1992 Hadrian Books Ltd became part of the BAR
group. This volume was originally published by Archaeopress in conjunction with
British Archaeological Reports (Oxford) Ltd / Hadrian Books Ltd, the Series principal
publisher, in 2006. This present volume is published by BAR Publishing, 2016.

Printed in England

BAR titles are available from:

          BAR Publishing
          122 Banbury Rd, Oxford, OX2 7BP, UK
EMAIL   info@barpublishing.com
PHONE +44 (0)1865 310431
FAX   +44 (0)1865 316916
          www.barpublishing.com

Contents

List of Figures ii
List of Tables iii
Contributors iv
Acknowledgements v
Summary vi

1. Introduction (*Joshua Pollard, Michael Hamilton & Neil Phillips*) 1
    1.1. The site and its setting 1
    1.2. Previous research and the context of the 2000 excavations 1

2. Excavation Results (*Joshua Pollard, Adrian Chadwick & Lesley McFadyen*) 6
    2.1. Methodology 6
    2.2. Trench 1: the interior 6
    2.3. Trench 2: the inner ditch and bank 18
    2.4. Trench 3: the western entrance 25

3. Artefactual Material 30
    3.1. Ironwork (*Philip Macdonald*) 31
    3.2. Metalworking slags (*Tim Young*) 32
    3.3. Prehistoric pottery (*Rick Peterson, Joshua Pollard & Elaine Morris*) 33
    3.4. Droitwich briquetage (*Joshua Pollard & Elaine Morris*) 37
    3.5. Roman pottery (*Ray Howell & Joshua Pollard*) 38
    3.6. Medieval pottery (*Rick Peterson & Joshua Pollard*) 38
    3.7. Brick and tile (*Joshua Pollard*) 38
    3.8. Fired clay (*Joshua Pollard*) 39
    3.9. Worked flint (*Joshua Pollard*) 40
    3.10. Other worked stone (*Joshua Pollard*) 40

4. Environmental Evidence (*Ruth Young*) 42
    4.1. Animal bone 42
    4.2. Charred plant remains and charcoal 42

5. Discussion: Lodge Hill Camp and the hillforts of Gwent
   (*Joshua Pollard, Ray Howell, Adrian Chadwick & Lesley McFadyen*) 47
    5.1. Later prehistoric activity and the creation of the hillfort 47
    5.2. Lodge Hill in its regional context 52
    5.3. Hillforts and social relations in south-east Wales 57
    5.4. The hillfort's relationship to the Legionary fortress 57
    5.5. Lodge Hill and hillfort re-occupation in south-east Wales during the late Roman/early medieval
        period 58

Appendix 1. Llanmelin Hillfort, Caerwent: geophysical and earthwork survey (*Daryl Williams*) 62

Bibliography 68

List of Figures

Figure 1. Lodge Hill and the hillforts of Gwent 2
Figure 2. Lodge Hill Camp from the south-west. Taken in July 1948 before tree cover obscured much of the interior and bank and ditch circuit. Cambridge University Collection of Air Photographs..........................3
Figure 3. Lodge Hill Camp. Earthwork plan showing the location of the 2000 excavations............................4
Figure 4. Coxe's 1801 plan of the 'Encampment of the Lodge' 4
Figure 5. Trench 1 under excavation, from the south-west...7
Figure 6. Trench 1. Phase 1 and Phase 2 features..8
Figure 7. Western end of Trench 1 on completion of excavation showing quarry hollow F.23, terrace F.24, and the Phase 2 rectangular structure (partially excavated), from the south-west..9
Figure 8. Western end of Trench 1 on completion of excavation with quarry hollow F.23 and post-hole F.21 in the foreground, from the south-east...9
Figure 9. Trench 1. Sections and profiles. Note that the top two sections show deposits after the removal of [001] and Phase 3 and 4 deposits. For location see figure 10 10
Figure 10. Trench 1. Location of sections (top) and the distribution of Iron Age artefacts (bottom)............11
Figure 11. Trench 1. Rectangular structure 12
Figure 12. Trench 1. Stony upper fill of ditch F.3 13
Figure 13. Trench 1. Phase 2 post-holes F.17, 18, 21, 22, 26 and 27 15
Figure 14. Trench 1. Base of post-hole F.17, from the north..16
Figure 15. Trench 1. Post-hole F.27 from the north 16
Figure 16. Trench 1. Phase 3 and Phase 4 features...17
Figure 17. Trench 1. Phase 3 terraces F.4 and 5, from the south 18
Figure 18. Trench 2 under excavation 19
Figure 19. Trench 2. Profile of inner bank (F.1) and ditch (F.16) 20
Figure 20. Trench 2. Bank under excavation 20
Figure 21. Trench 2. East-facing section of bank 22
Figure 22. Trench 2. East-facing bank section..23
Figure 23. Trench 2. East facing section of ditch 24
Figure 24. Trench 2. East-facing ditch section. Note that the steps on the left-hand side are a product of excavation...25
Figure 25. Trench 3, western entrance. South-facing section (top) and plan of bank deposits and pit F.42 on completion of excavation (bottom)...26
Figure 26. Trench 3. Section CD showing bank deposits and later re-cut of entrance (cut [152])...............27
Figure 27. Trench 3. East end of entrance on completion of excavation, showing area of 'guard chamber' 28
Figure 28. Metalwork: 1. loop-headed spike (Trench 1, [002]); 2. possible joiner's dog (Trench 1, [011]); 3. La Tène I brooch (Trench 1, F.3, [027])...32
Figure 29. Iron Age pottery (1-11) and briquetage (12-13). 36
Figure 30. Roman pottery 39
Figure 31. Worked stone: 1, 3. grooved slabs (Trench 1, [002]); 2. hammerstone/pounder (Trench 1, [002]); 4-5. flaked discs (Trench 1, [010]) 41
Figure 32. 'Guard chamber' arrangements at Lodge Hill (conjectural reconstruction based on Trench 3 features) and Dinorben (after Gardner & Savory 1964)..50
Figure 33. Excavated Gwent hillforts 53
Figure 34. Sudbrook Camp. Features revealed through excavation and geophysical survey (after Nash-Williams 1939 and Sell 2001)...55
Figure 35. Phases of activity at excavated Gwent hillforts 56
Figure 36. Llanmelin. Earthwork survey 63
Figure 37. Llanmelin Main Entrance. Evidence of phasing (after Nash-Williams 1939).............................64
Figure 38. Llanmelin. Magnetometer survey (top) and interpretation of geophysical survey results (bottom)..........66

List of Tables

Table 1. Details of Phase 2 post-holes 14
Table 2. Summary of finds according to context 30
Table 3. Prehistoric pottery according to fabric and context 34
Table 4. Prehistoric pottery from Trench 1 according to fabric and phase 35
Table 5. Droitwich briquetage according to context, phase and fabric 38
Table 6. Fired clay according to context and fabric 40
Table 7. Calcined animal bone: quantities and identification 42
Table 8. Summary of presence of wood charcoal in all samples processed 43
Table 9. Wood charcoal identifications 45

Contributors

CHADWICK, HAMILTON, HOWELL, LEAVER, PHILLIPS, WILLIAMS:
School of Humanities & Science
University of Wales, Newport
Caerleon Campus
PO Box 179
Newport, NP18 3YG

MACDONALD:
Centre for Archaeological Fieldwork
School of Archaeology and Palaeoecology
The Queen's University of Belfast
Belfast, BT7 1NN

MCFADYEN:
School of Archaeology & Ancient History
University of Leicester
University Road
Leicester, LE1 7RH

MORRIS:
Archaeology
University of Southampton
Avenue Campus
Highfield
Southampton, SO17 1BF

PETERSON:
School of Natural Resources
University of Central Lancashire
Preston, PR1 2HE

POLLARD:
Dept. of Archaeology & Anthropology
University of Bristol
43 Woodland Road
Bristol, BS8 1UU

YOUNG, R.:
School of Archaeology & Ancient History
University of Leicester
University Road
Leicester, LE1 7RH

YOUNG, T.:
GeoArch
54 Heol y Cadno
Thornhill
Cardiff, CF14 9DY

Acknowledgements

The June-July 2000 excavations at Lodge Hill were initiated and fully-funded by the Charles Williams' Charity of Caerleon as a Millennium project. Mr D.R. Prosser and the Lodge Hill Church and Glyn Jones of Lodge Farm kindly granted access to the site. Scheduled Monument Consent was granted by Cadw (Welsh Historic Monuments) on behalf of the National Assembly for Wales; and we wish particularly to thank Dr Mike Yates for overseeing the application and providing valuable comment on the initial project design. The excavations were directed by the authors with supervisory assistance from Ian Dennis, Mike Hamilton, Lesley McFadyen and Steve O'Rourke. Anne Leaver assisted with much of the pre-excavation organisation. Much of the hard work was undertaken by volunteers and students from the University of Wales College, Newport: Stuart Abbott, Nicki Baird, Hayley Barton, Adam Darnborough, Kevin Davies, Tracey Davies, Kelly Davies, Kelly Dixon, Gail Giles, Lenny Griffen, Carolyn Haggett, Kathryn Hyde, Iestyn Jones, Matthew Mathias, Sally Perrett, Rebecca Power, Sally Preece, Emma Pritchard, Simon Rathore, John Roberts, Christopher Seaman, Georgina Spear, Jon Tanner, Mike Thomas, Martin Tuck, David Vaughan. Neil Phillips and Kate Smith battled through thick vegetation in order to produce a fine earthwork survey. Helpful insights and assistance with the post-excavation work have been provided by Mark Bowden, Adam Gwilt, Jeremy Knight, Grahame Makepeace, Elaine Morris, Peter Webster and David Zienkiewicz.

Philip Macdonald gratefully acknowledges the assistance of Adam Gwilt, Phil Parkes and Siobhan Stevenson in the study of the ironwork.

Daryl Williams wishes to thank Cadw for their permission to carry out fieldwork at Llanmelin; Dr. Mike Hamilton for his assistance with the geophysical survey and processing the results; and staff at the University of Wales Newport for their encouragement and support. Thanks are also due to Adam Gwilt and staff of the National Museum and Galleries of Wales who made available for study the documentation and material culture from the 1930s excavations of Nash-Williams. Special thanks also to Sam Williams who was present throughout the fieldwork and whose contribution was invaluable. Finally this report would not have been possible without the hard work and assistance of Mark Belcher, Rodger Burchill, Jonathon Burton, Jane Harris, Gill Levy, Ian McFarlane and Dave Rogers.

Summary

This volume describes work on the Iron Age hillfort of Lodge Hill Camp, in Gwent, south-east Wales. Situated adjacent to the later Roman legionary fortress at Caerleon, the hillfort has, until recently, received little archaeological attention. Excavation was undertaken during the summer of 2000 within the interior of the hillfort, at its western entrance, and across the inner bank and ditch of the defences. Though limited in scale, the results of this work suggest the first phase of hillfort dates to the 5th century BC. During the middle or late Iron Age additional circuits of defence were added, some of these with V-shaped ditches and dump ramparts. At this stage the western entrance was blocked, and the eastern entrance probably elaborated.

Excavation within the interior revealed a substantial quarry hollow and a series of rock-cut scoops/platforms. Post-holes indicated the presence of timber structures, at least one of which was rectangular. A small ditched enclosure was created within the interior at an early stage, and may have served to define an area utilised for iron-working. Associated with the timber structures and enclosure were a small quantity of ironwork, including a fine La Tène I brooch, pottery, briquetage, worked stone and burnt animal bone. The pottery includes vessels in Malvernian area fabrics, while the Droitwich briquetage extends the previously known distribution of these containers by c.15-20km. Occupation need not have been permanent.

During the late Iron Age occupation within the western part of the hillfort appeared to cease, and a series of narrow terraces were laid out across this area. There was renewed occupation, albeit on a small-scale, in the early centuries AD; a small assemblage of predominantly late Roman pottery being associated with a lightly-built timber structure. Parts of the inner rampart either collapsed or were deliberately slighted during the period of Roman occupation. There remains the tantalising possibility of early Medieval use of the site, seen perhaps with the creation of a small oval enclosure within the former hillfort ramparts and the reinstating of the western entrance.

An extended discussion is offered of Lodge Hill's position within the regional Iron Age sequence, and of Roman and early Medieval reuse of hillforts in south Wales. The results of geophysical and earthwork survey at the hillfort of Llanmelin, near Chepstow, are also reported on.

1. Introduction

Joshua Pollard, Michael Hamilton & Neil Phillips

1.1. The Site and its Setting

Lodge Hill (or Lodge Wood) Camp is an imposing hillfort situated on the north-west edge of present day Caerleon, Gwent (ST 323914)(Fig. 1). The site occupies a dominant and commanding position on a ridge of Old Red Sandstone, overlooking the city of Newport, the mouth of the Usk valley and the eastern reach of the Severn estuary. The highest part of the hill, at its western end, reaches 120m OD. To the north-west, and to a lesser extent south, the side of the hill drops steeply from the summit of the ridge, whereas the approaches from the south-west and east are characterised by more gentle inclines. The River Usk runs past the foot of the hill c.0.75km to the south; the hillfort being positioned close to a major bend in the river as it changes from an ENE-WSW to north-south course. The setting of the hillfort is now spoiled somewhat by the encroachment of modern housing up the southern flanks of the hill, to within 100m of the earthworks.

The hillfort comprises a triple-banked enclosure c.400 x 200m in extent, aligned along the crest of the hill, and enclosing an area of c.2.2ha (Figs 2 & 3). For the most part, the earthworks remain well-defined, particularly in the western half of the monument where they have suffered less from later building and agricultural activity. There is an original entrance into the site at its western end, and another almost certainly existed in the south-east corner of the monument where a modern track leads to the buildings of Lodge Farm. The western entrance has a complex structural history (see below), with an early phase of blocking then redefinition at a much later date. That at the south-east probably functioned as the main entrance for much of the life of the hillfort. On the south, west and north there are additional lengths of bank and ditch: that on the north deviating from the course of the main ramparts; while the additional stretch of bank on the south appears to 'spiral out' from the main outer rampart in the area of the western entrance (Fig. 3). Another anomalous feature is a 100m length of bank sandwiched between the second and third rampart near the western end of the south side. Of lesser dimensions, this has the appearance of an earlier phase of rampart that was subsequently incorporated into a massive elaboration of the defences on the south side – in its final form comprising a total of five lines of bank and ditch with a depth of nearly 90m from exterior to interior. A smaller and very regular univallate oval enclosure (c.100 x 50m across) lies within the western third of the hillfort interior. Both its eastern and western ends are rounded, the latter corresponding to the course of the main inner rampart. Entrance gaps are present on both ends of the enclosure. It remains uncertain whether the inner enclosure pre- or post-dates the hillfort. Such complexity in the visible earthwork remains implies several phases of construction (Whittle 1992, 45).

1.2. Previous research and the context of the 2000 excavations

Despite its size, and position adjacent to the Roman legionary fortress at Caerleon, the monument has attracted little archaeological interest. The earliest detailed plan and written description of the monument appears to be that of William Coxe, compiled for his *An Historical Tour of Monmouthshire* (1801):

> The most remarkable of these is the encampment of the Lodge, in the old park of Lantarnam, near a mile to the north-west of Caerleon, anciently called BELLINGSTOCKE, which is supposed by Harris to have been the æstiva or summer camp of the second legion: it is of an oval, or rather an elliptical shape, large dimensions, and surrounded with double ramparts, excepting to the south-west, where there [is] a quadruple line of ramparts and ditches. The entrenchments are in some places not less than thirty feet in depth. The entrance is to the west, and defended by a tumulus, twelve yards in height, which is placed on the inner rampart. It bears more the appearance of a British, than of a Roman encampment; and if I may be allowed a conjecture, was the site of the British town on the arrival of the Romans. (Coxe 1801, 90)

The accompanying engraving (Coxe 1801, pl. V7) shows the flattened eastern end of the hillfort, the position of the Lodge on the line of the outer bank and ditch, and one major and several minor gaps through the defences on the south-east side (Fig. 4). Levelling of the earthworks on the south-east had clearly taken place prior to Coxe's visit, and may have been associated with the creation of farm buildings here during the early post-medieval period.

The 1833 Ordnance Survey shows the hillfort as a 'tombstone' shaped earthwork with a very regular straight eastern end. At this side, not only do the buildings of Lodge Farm appear to cut through the ramparts, but there are also two approach lanes. The south-east lane remains today, but that from the north-east was absent by 1886. The 1886 OS map shows more intrusion by the farm buildings into the south-east rampart, with the complete

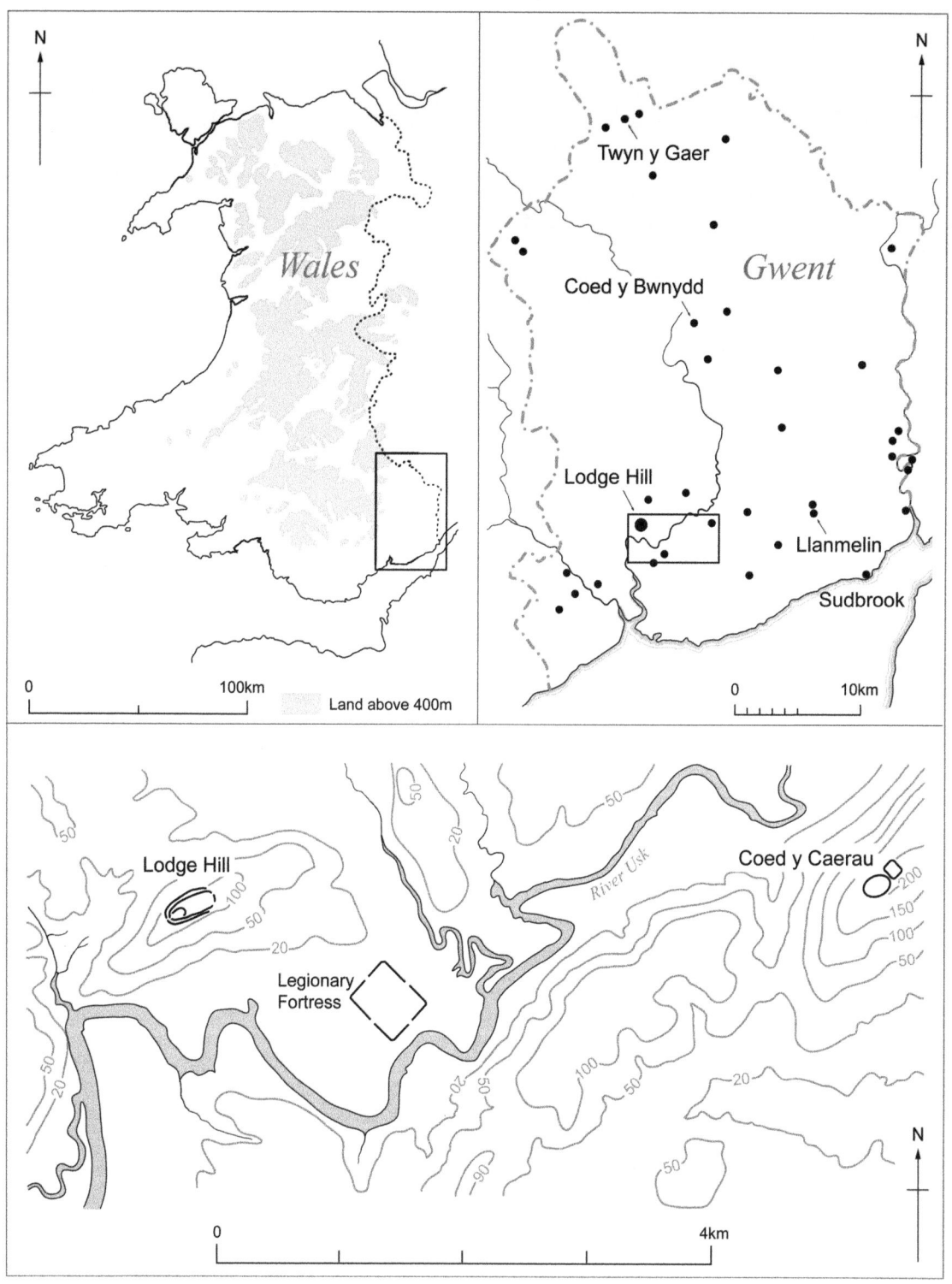

FIGURE 1. LODGE HILL AND THE HILLFORTS OF GWENT

FIGURE 2. LODGE HILL CAMP FROM THE SOUTH-WEST. TAKEN IN JULY 1948 BEFORE TREE COVER OBSCURED MUCH OF THE INTERIOR AND BANK AND DITCH CIRCUIT. CAMBRIDGE UNIVERSITY COLLECTION OF AIR PHOTOGRAPHS

removal of ramparts and ditches on this side. The site, along with other Gwent hillforts, was surveyed by E.A. Downman in 1910, though his unpublished plan is schematic and shows little additional detail (we are grateful to Caroline Martin for drawing our attention to the existence of this survey).

An opportunity to examine the site arose in 2000 with the offer of a generous grant from a Caerleon-based educational body, the Charles Williams' Charity. As part of a millennium project, the Trust agreed to fund both the excavation itself and post-excavation analysis. Consent for the work was kindly granted by Cadw, Welsh Historic Monuments. Prior to the 2000 excavations, very little was known about the monument. It was uncertain, for example, when the earliest phases of the hillfort were constructed, the period of time over which it was used, and whether occupation of any scale took place within the interior. Within a broader context, it was anticipated that the excavation could enhance our understanding of the nature of Iron Age settlement and landscape organisation in the Gwent region (cf. Howell & Pollard 2004). The hillfort also lies within close proximity to the Roman legionary fortress at Caerleon (Boon 1987) – in fact, the two sites are intervisible – which raised interesting questions about the interaction between Roman and indigenous communities at the time of the Roman conquest. Was the hillfort occupied at the time of the conquest, and if so, was there evidence of Roman military take-over or continued occupation? Furthermore, could

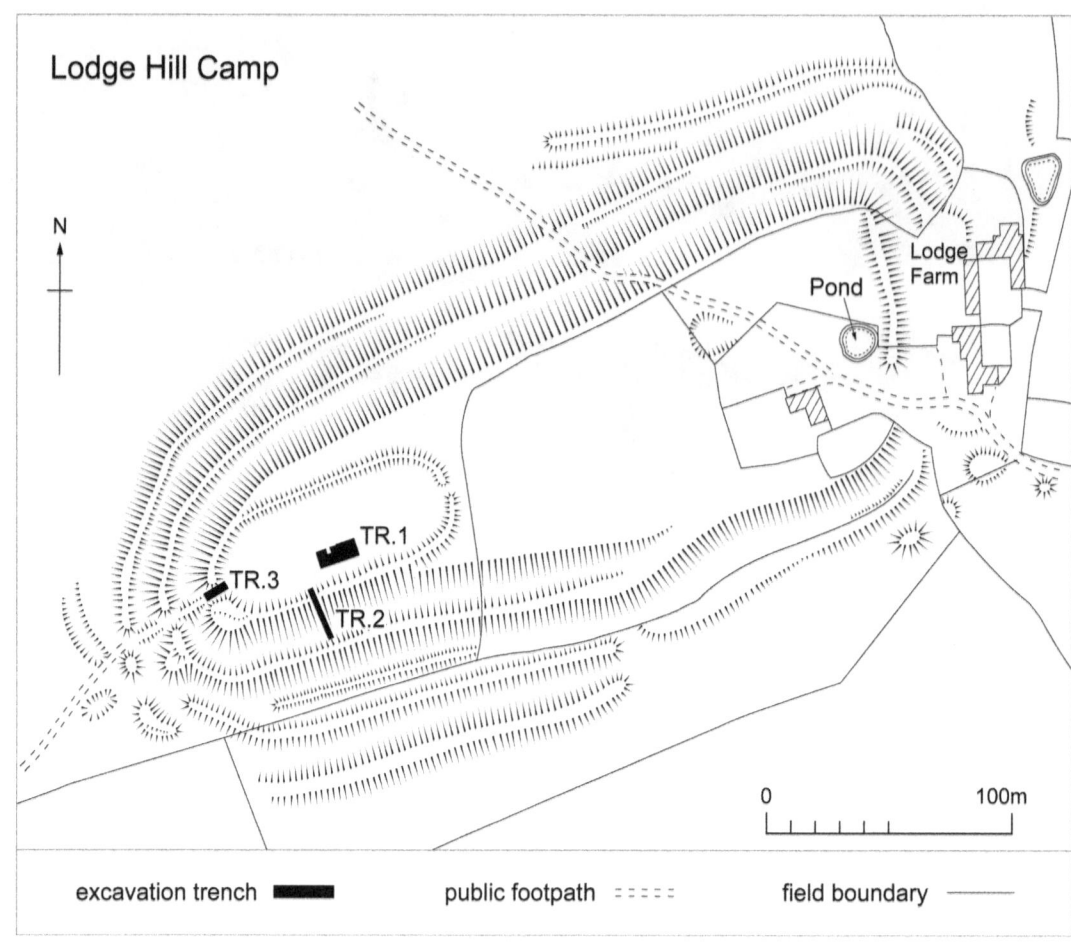

FIGURE 3. LODGE HILL CAMP. EARTHWORK PLAN SHOWING THE LOCATION OF THE 2000 EXCAVATIONS

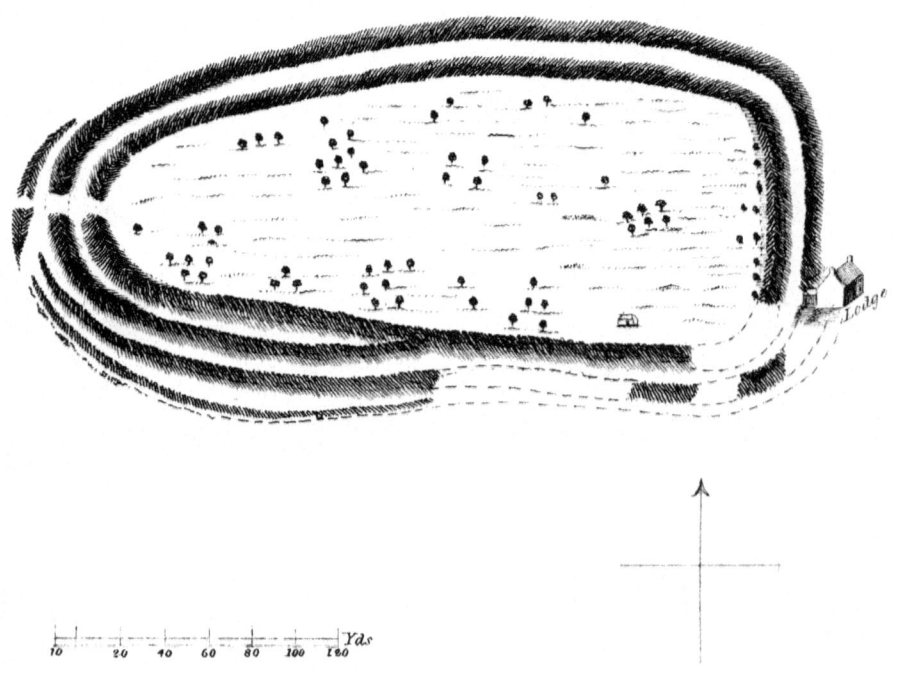

FIGURE 4. COXE'S 1801 PLAN OF THE 'ENCAMPMENT OF THE LODGE'

the hillfort, like many other sites of this kind in Wales and western Britain (Dark 1994), have been the focus for re-occupation during the late Roman and/or early medieval periods?

The key aims of the excavation were therefore to establish:

- enhanced understanding of the date and sequence of rampart construction
- the character of activity within the interior of the hillfort (e.g. occupation, agricultural storage, craft activity, etc)
- whether evidence existed for pre- and post-hillfort activity (Neolithic, Bronze Age, Roman and/or post-Roman), and the form that this might take.

2. Excavation Results
Joshua Pollard, Adrian Chadwick & Lesley McFadyen

Given the presence of the small inner enclosure and an apparently undisturbed original entrance, targeted investigation within the western half of the hillfort appeared to offer the best opportunity to establish sequences of construction and activity with limited intervention. Prior to excavation (May 2000), a geophysical survey was undertaken over a small area (20 x 10m) of the western sector of the interior by Dr Michael Hamilton. The survey was greatly hampered by the dense vegetation covering this part of the site, and the results were largely inconclusive. Poor management of the site since the Second World War has led to the establishment of very dense tree and scrub growth. Not only has this obscured much of the archaeology, but it has led to quite extensive root damage to deposits within the interior (see below).

2.1. Methodology
Excavation took place over a period of four weeks in June and early July 2000. Three areas were designated for investigation. Trench 1 defined an area of 106m^2 within the western third of the interior, close to the southern rampart. Trench 2 (21 x 2m) was placed across the first (inner) line of bank and ditch adjacent to the south-west of Trench 1; while Trench 3 (an area of c.30m^2) was sited over the northern bank terminal and passageway of the innermost section of the western entrance (Fig. 3). Additional small-scale interventions were made in and around areas of mountain bike damage within the western entrance. All excavation was undertaken by hand.

Excavation recording followed a modified version of the Museum of London (MoLAS) single context system, though adherence to single context *planning* was not deemed necessary for this particular work. Excavated stratigraphic entities (e.g. a cut, layer or fill) were recorded as individual contexts, numbered sequentially ([001] onwards). Interrelated stratigraphic units (e.g. a ditch and its fill) were assigned feature numbers (F.1 onwards). Drawn sections were made at 1:10 and 1:20, and base plans and feature plans at 1:20. A full photographic record was kept, although poor lighting conditions under a thick canopy of tree-cover often made photography difficult.

Finds were collected and bagged according to context, with details of feature, context and finds number (sequentially numbered <001> onwards) recorded on the bag. Whenever possible individual finds were three-dimensionally recorded.

The results of the excavation are summarized according to trench.

2.2. Trench 1: the interior
Within the confines of the main rampart and ditch system and the smaller inner enclosure, Trench 1 was positioned 45m back from the western entrance, on the south-facing slope of the natural ridge that defines the western extent of the hilltop. Here, the ground sloped on a north-west – south-east incline, more steeply on the east (1:7) than the west (1:10). At this point the interior has noticeably narrowed in comparison to areas to the east – 50m overall, but only 30m across as defined by the inner enclosure. It was originally intended to excavate a 20 x 10m area, but dense tree cover severely restricted the extent of excavation (Fig. 5). However, the reduction in the area of the trench proved fortuitous, since the deposits encountered here were both deeper and more complex than anticipated. For this reason, only selected areas within the trench, principally in its western half, were subject to total excavation.

It is important to stress from the outset the difficulties encountered in the excavation of this area, which have a considerable impact upon the interpretation of the archaeological sequence revealed. Intensive biological activity, in particular tree and scrub root action, had resulted in severe reworking of the soil matrices, effectively removing obvious boundaries between originally discrete layers and deposits. Consequently, it was often impossible to determine context changes in the normal way, that is on the basis of macroscopically visible variations in soil structure, colour and composition. In nearly all instances stratigraphic boundaries and feature fills were identified by changes in stone density. This meant that normal stratigraphic excavation was not always possible. Deposits within the area had often to be excavated in arbitrary spits, and the soil removed from around the stony fills of ditches and post-holes in order to define their presence and extent. Many features (certainly stake-holes, but also pits and gullies with stone-free fills) may not have been detected because of this extensive biological reworking of the soil. An added problem, common to many sites in the region, was the acidic nature of the sandstone-derived soils, which had led to the destruction of unburnt bone and perhaps some ceramic material and more fragile metalwork.

The deposits are described according to phase. Necessarily, the phasing is to some extent arbitrary, being

FIGURE 5. TRENCH 1 UNDER EXCAVATION, FROM THE SOUTH-WEST

defined according to observed structural changes, which may or may not relate to major transformations in the way in which the site was used and inhabited.

Phase 1: The quarry hollow and terraces
The sequence begins with the cutting of a linear quarry (F.23) in the lee of the inner bank, and further up-slope two adjacent scoops/terraces (F.24 (west) and F.25 (east)). All were cut into the sandstone bedrock (Fig. 6).

The quarry F.23 [154] ran at a slightly oblique angle (east-west) across the length of the trench, and continued beyond at both ends. Its width ranged from over 4.8m at the west to over 2.0m at the east; its southern edge lying outside the excavated area. The base and sides were uneven. Its depth varied from 0.8m against the western section, rising to 0.5m in the centre of the trench, then markedly dipping to 1.0m just to the east of this. The stone had evidently been prised out along natural bedding planes, resulting in an irregular and stepped base sloping to the south (Figs 7-10). The top edge made expedient use of an interface between a band of clay marl (perhaps decayed limestone) and solid rock, creating a straight northern edge along its central section. Elsewhere the sides varied from steep to shallow. Lying within the lee of the inner bank and apparently following its course, the feature was almost certainly dug to obtain stone for bank construction.

The rock-cut scoops F.24 [155] and 25 [156] were worked into the slope of the hill to the north of F.23 (Fig. 6). No direct stratigraphic relationship could be established between the quarry hollow and scoops, but they are here assumed to be more or less contemporary. Both scoops were of similar dimensions: 6.0 and 5.8+m across and over 1.8m wide, with parts extending beyond the excavated area. They were highly irregular in plan, probably resulting from the difficulty experienced in quarrying the sandstone bedrock in any regular fashion. F.24 was up to 0.6m deep, being deepest on the south where the base followed down the bedding plane of the rock. The exposed portion of F.25 was not fully excavated, only being taken to the base in one sondage in the western half of the feature. Here, it was up to 0.8m deep, the base again sloping down to the south.

The quarry hollow and scoops may have begun to silt-up soon after being dug, in some cases that process being augmented by deliberate backfill. On the west side of F.23 a discrete thin layer of purple-brown clay loam [048], c.1.4m across, overlay the base of the quarry. Perhaps an occupation soil, this contained few stones, frequent charcoal and four fragments of Droitwich briquetage. Covering this and filling the west section of the quarry was a similar soil [042]/[037] with varying quantities of stone and some charcoal flecking, in places up to 0.4m deep. A small quantity of Iron Age pottery, briquetage and fired clay came from this soil. Elsewhere, the fill was an homogenous purple-brown loam [011] up to 0.6m deep. This contained occasional stone,

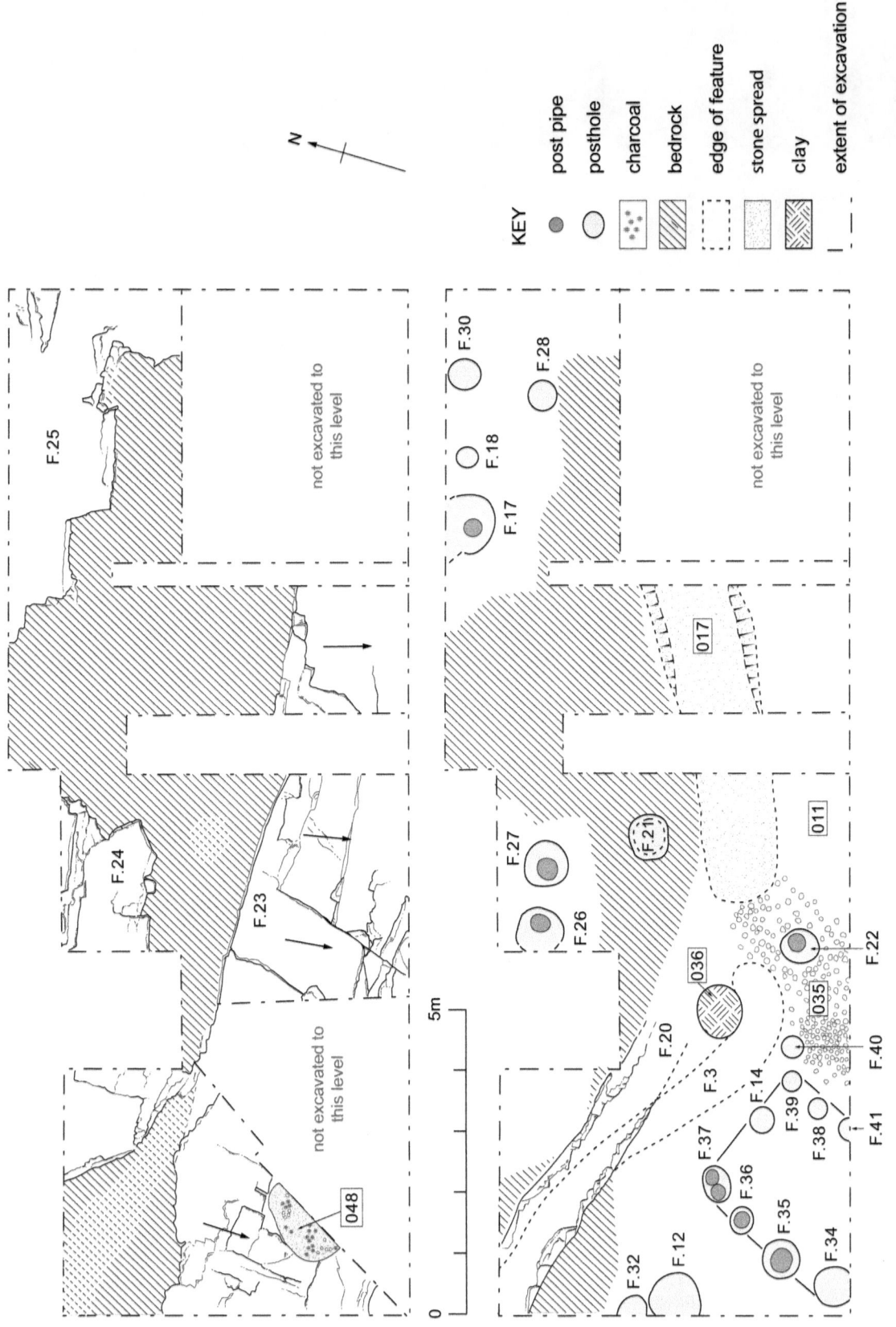

FIGURE 6. TRENCH 1. PHASE 1 (TOP) AND PHASE 2 (BOTTOM) FEATURES

FIGURE 7. WESTERN END OF TRENCH 1 ON COMPLETION OF EXCAVATION SHOWING QUARRY HOLLOW F.23, TERRACE F.24, AND THE PHASE 2 RECTANGULAR STRUCTURE (PARTIALLY EXCAVATED), FROM THE SOUTH-WEST

FIGURE 8. WESTERN END OF TRENCH 1 ON COMPLETION OF EXCAVATION WITH QUARRY HOLLOW F.23 AND POST-HOLE F.21 IN THE FOREGROUND, FROM THE SOUTH-EAST

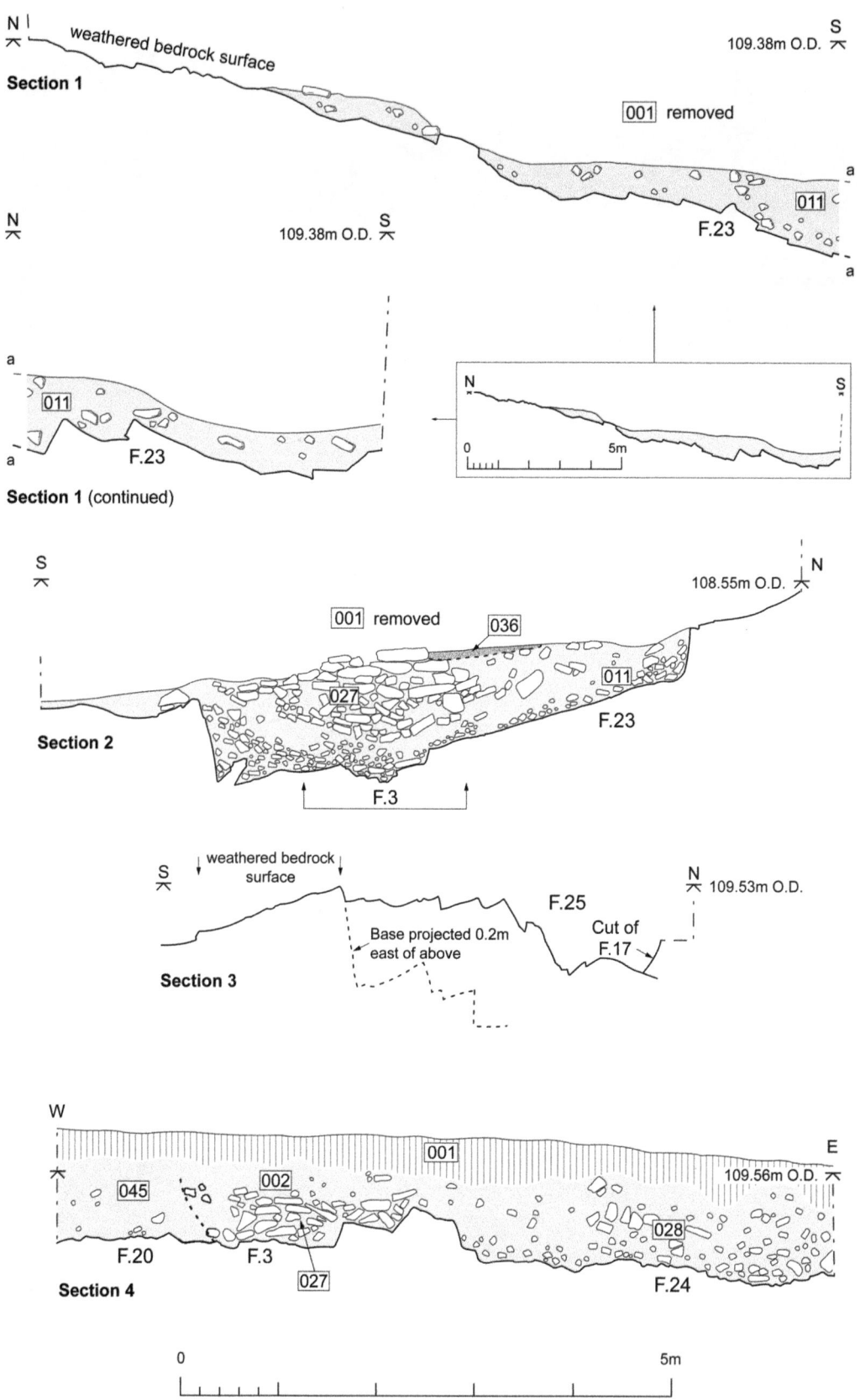

FIGURE 9. TRENCH 1. SECTIONS AND PROFILES. NOTE THAT THE TOP TWO SECTIONS SHOW DEPOSITS AFTER THE REMOVAL OF [001] AND PHASE 3 AND 4 DEPOSITS. FOR LOCATION SEE FIGURE 10

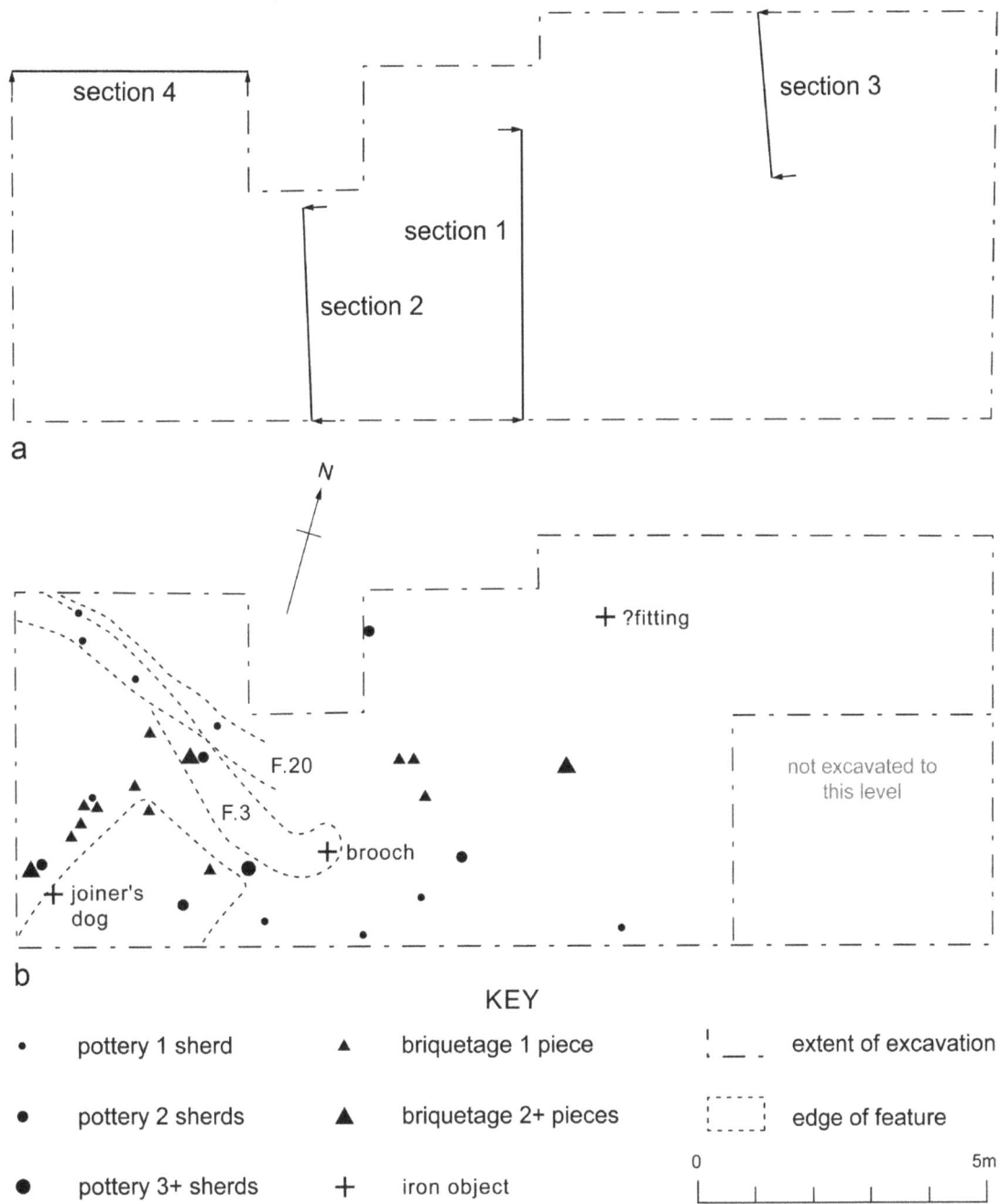

FIGURE 10. TRENCH 1. LOCATION OF SECTIONS (TOP) AND THE DISTRIBUTION OF IRON AGE ARTEFACTS (BOTTOM)

particularly towards the base and sides where it probably formed a primary weathering deposit. An iron joiner's dog was recovered from [011], along with 16 sherds of middle Iron Age pottery, three pieces of briquetage, a stone pounder and rubber, and fragments of fired clay.

F.25 and the eastern half of F.24 were filled with a stony purple-brown clay loam, [010] and [038] respectively, the latter being paler and pinkish towards the base with a greater content of stone. Diffuse charcoal spreads and small quantities of metalworking debris were noted in both fills. A few sherds of pottery, a possible iron dome-headed stud and two flaked stone discs were recovered from [010]. In contrast, the western half of F.24 contained a densely packed spread of angular sandstone [028]. The stones within this matrix were set at various angles, some being steeply pitched, almost vertical. Although some of the steeply-pitched slabs could represent post-packing, these did not resolve themselves into discrete features upon further excavation. In fact, the area of [028] may have suffered considerable root-disturbance, in the process destroying any structure in the stone spread. Unfortunately, the relationship between [028] and [038] could not be established because of the presence of an intervening baulk, the position of which was dictated by the presence of several small trees.

Phase 2: the inner enclosure and post structures
Resting on and cut into the fill of the quarry and scoops were a series of features that may relate to a phase of more intensive occupation within this part of the hillfort. These comprise cobble and stone surfaces, a small rectangular structure, a number of post-settings and two shallow ditches that might describe one side of a small enclosure within the interior of the hillfort (Fig. 6). This phase is dated to the middle Iron Age on the basis of associated ceramics and metalwork. The excavation of deposits at this level was largely restricted to the western two-thirds of the trench.

In the south-western corner of the trench a setting of eight post-holes enclosing an irregularly paved area defined a small rectilinear building (Fig. 11). Aligned NNE-SSW, as exposed the structure was 2.2m wide and at least 3.0m long. The western side of the building was defined by a slightly bowed line of four post-holes (F.34-7), the eastern by a similar line of three (F.38-9, 41), and the northern end by a single post-hole (F.14) just offset to one side of the structure's axis. If the structure's full length is given by the exposed western side and it is symmetrical along its axis, then ten earth-fast posts in all would have been employed in its construction. The post-holes were largely defined by the presence of stone packing in their upper profiles; typically for the site the cuts being largely invisible in the reworked soil matrix. Only those forming the western wall of the structure were excavated, and details of their dimensions are given in Table 1. Enclosed within the post settings was an irregular paved surface [033]. The latter comprised angular and sub-angular sandstone pieces, tightly set to form a slightly undulating surface, dipping towards the middle. Larger blocks had been used along the western edge, where they had been packed against standing posts. Some of tabular blocks were sizeable slabs, being in excess of 0.6m across, while within the centre of the floor was one particularly large piece 0.7m across. Beyond cleaning and definition, the floor surface was not further explored. However, there were no signs of an internal hearth, nor of floor deposits typical of occupation, suggesting that the structure served an ancillary function. The only associated finds were two sherds of pottery and a few fragments of fired clay.

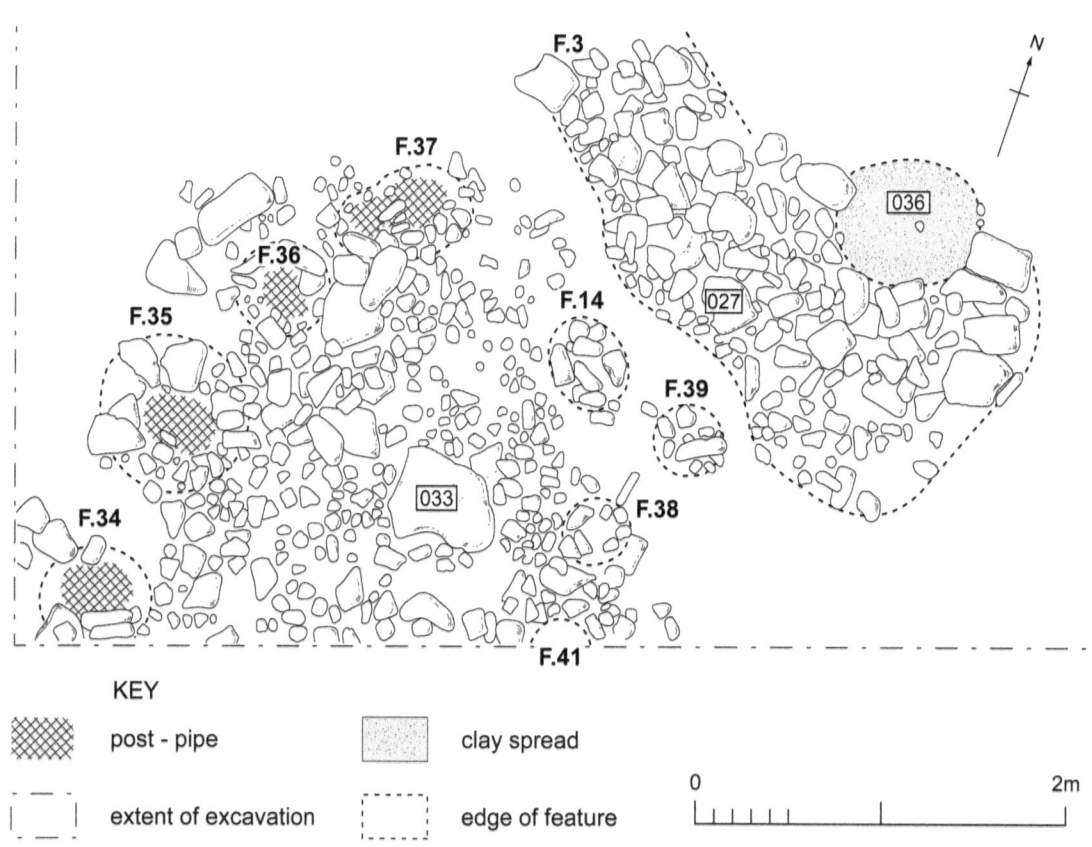

FIGURE 11. TRENCH 1. RECTANGULAR STRUCTURE

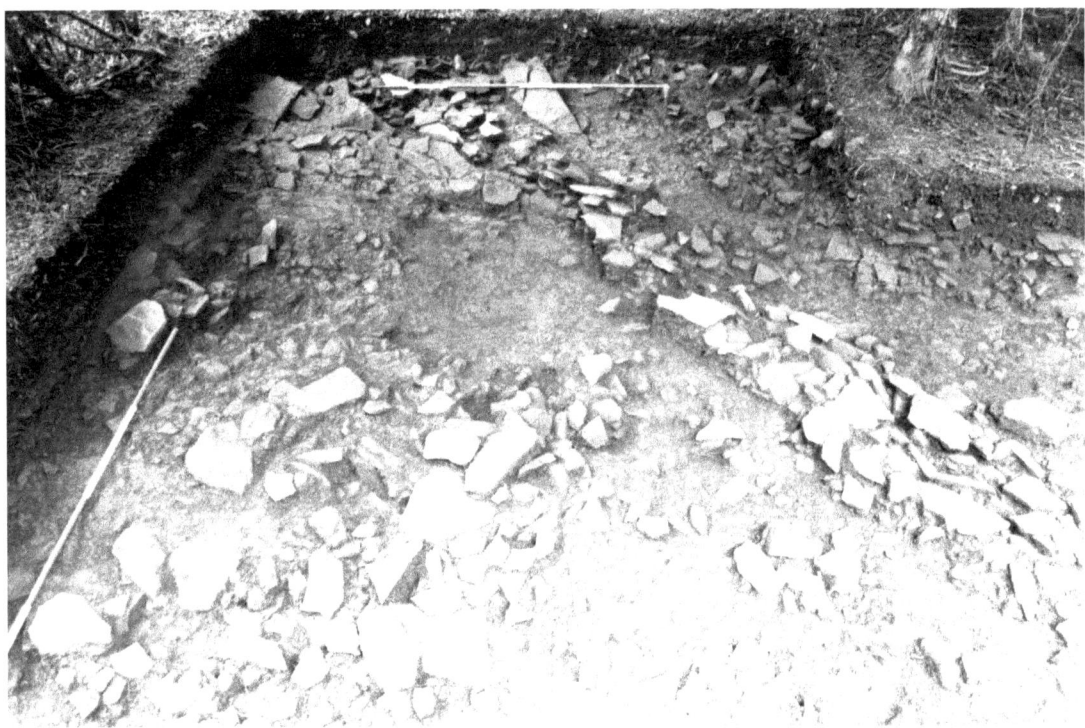

FIGURE 12. TRENCH 1. STONY UPPER FILL OF DITCH F.3

The rectangular structure was constructed immediately south of two inter-cutting shallow ditches, F.3 and 20, which ran roughly NW-SE from the north-west corner of the excavated area (Fig. 12). They were traced over a distance of 6-7m, both apparently terminating within the fill of the quarry hollow F.23, although by this stage it was extremely difficult to detect cuts. Both ditches followed similar, though not identical, courses. F.20 [047] was the earliest. 0.5-0.7m wide and c.0.4m deep (as excavated), it had steep to near vertical sides and a flat base. It was cut into the bedrock over most of its length, and ran diagonally across the north-south slope of this part of the site. It was filled with a purple-brown clay loam [045], containing more stone towards the base. The ditch line was then redefined by the cutting of F.3 [046]. This followed a slightly different and more sinuous alignment, particularly at its eastern end where it had a markedly in-turned terminal. Its extent could be defined quite closely by the stony upper fill [027]. The ditch cut was c.0.7m wide and 0.2-0.4m deep, being deepest at the terminal end. Where cut through the rock it possessed a flat base. The upper fill [027] consisted of a deposit of angular sandstone rubble, with individual blocks up to 0.4m across; many of the larger blocks occurring at the terminal end. This stony deposit was more intermittent in the north-western section of the ditch where two separate 'dumps', each c.1.5m across, were visible. The stone spread clearly represents a deliberate backfill event, though curiously this material was 'layered' rather than angled (which would be expected had it simply been tipped in), suggesting the whole backfilling process was carefully executed. The stone used in the backfill process must have been brought from elsewhere on site, since over much of its exposed course the ditch was cut through earlier, largely stone-free, feature fills. Given that the stony upper fill of F.3 was visible at a slightly higher level than the surface of the rectangular structure, this phase of ditch most probably post-dates the structure. Perhaps a deliberate deposit, an iron La Tène I brooch was found in the eastern terminal of F.3. Twelve sherds of pottery from a single jar and two pieces of briquetage were also found in the fill of this feature (Fig. 10, bottom).

Situated within the in-turned terminal of F.3 was a localised patch of compact orange-brown clay loam [036]. Roughly oval, 0.6 x 0.7m across and only c.0.02m thick, this contained frequent charcoal flecks and small fragments of burnt sandstone. It most probably represents the base of a hearth, although it cannot be connected with any particular structure.

A number of artificially created surfaces and spreads of stone were identified at the same level as the structure, ditches and hearth. More apparent in section than in plan, to the west of the rectangular building was a diffuse spread of stone, including several horizontally-set tabular blocks [165]. In the area around and immediately to the east of the rectangular structure and ditches F.3 and 20 was a densely packed spread of sub-angular and rounded sandstone cobbles [035], forming a slightly uneven surface. This apparently butted against or went under a more extensive east-west stone and soil spread [017] that ran across the central southern area of the trench. 1.5m wide and curving slightly to the north; this was made up of small and medium sized sandstone pieces, pitched a

	Diameter	Depth	Comments
Within terrace F.25:			
F.17 [062], [039], [040]	1.00x0.80m	0.50m	Post-pipe 0.35m diameter
F.18 [041]	0.40x0.30m	-	Status as post-hole uncertain
F.28 [073]	0.90x70m	-	Status as post-hole uncertain
F.30 [078]	0.60x0.50m	-	Not excavated
Within terrace F.24:			
F.26 [071]	0.70m	c.0.25m	Post-pipe 0.3m diameter
F.27 [072]	0.80m	c.0.40m	Post-pipe 0.3m diameter
Central and western area:			
F.12 [026]	c.0.80	0.40m	
F.21 [052], [051]	0.90x0.80m	c.0.35m	
F.22 [054], [053]	0.60m	0.50m	Post-pipe 0.25m diameter
F.32 [157]	c.0.50	0.30m	
F.40 [164]	c.0.4m	-	Not excavated
Rectilinear structure:			
F.14 [029]	c.0.5m	-	Not excavated
F.34 [049]	c.0.6m	c.0.3m	Post-pipe c0.20m diameter
F.35 [159]	c.0.8m	c.0.5m	Post-pipe 0.40m diameter
F.36 [160]	c.0.7m	c.0.5m	Post-pipe 0.30m diameter
F.37 [161]	c.0.5m	c.0.5m	Double post-pipe? Both c.0.20 diameter
F.38 [162]	c.0.4m	-	Not excavated
F.39 [163]	c.0.4m		Not excavated
F.41 [166]	c.0.2m+	-	Not excavated

TABLE 1. DETAILS OF PHASE 2 POST-HOLES.

various angles in a loose matrix with numerous voids. In places the stones formed quite a dense layer, and lenses of smaller stones often overlay coarser 'rubble'. Rather than being a surface *per se*, [017] is likely to be the remnants of an up-cast bank. Its edge was very well defined on the south-east side, perhaps indicating the former presence of revetting or an accompanying ditch. If soil filled, the cut and fill of such a ditch would have been indistinguishable from the soil matrix of the quarry hollow into which it was dug. The presence of such a feature could explain the absence of post-holes in this area. Furthermore, [017] and the putative ditch could be seen to represent an easterly continuation of the F.3/20 ditch line, defining one side of a small enclosure with a narrow southerly entrance paved by spread [035].

In addition to those of the rectangular structure, a number of other post-holes were identified which can broadly be assigned to this phase (Table 1). There were obvious difficulties in defining these features, especially where cut into the soil matrices of the backfilled quarry hollow and scoops. With the exception of F.21, which was cut into the bedrock (as was the base of F.17), all other post-holes were dug through soil matrices where cut interfaces were no longer discernable, and were therefore identified by the presence of stone packing (Fig. 13). Post-holes with little or no stone packing, if they existed, would have been impossible to detect, as would stake-holes. There is some sequence to these features in as much as F.12, against the western end of the trench, could be shown to be later than F.32. F.22 projected, or cut, through surface [035].

F.12, 21, 22, 30, 32 and 38 were packed around with vertical and/or steeply pitched slabs. More elaborately constructed were some of the larger post-holes in the central and eastern half of the trench, F.17, 21, 26 and 27 (Figs 14 & 15). The packing for F.17 comprised vertical and pitched slabs set around the base of the post, some of these being sizeable (0.2-0.3m); while the upper part of the packing consisted of tightly-packed smaller stone pieces, sometimes laid horizontally, and evidently filling the entire space between the post and pit sides. That of F.21, 26 and 27 was similar. In most instances post-pipes were identifiable as cores of loose soil and small stones. The inward collapse of packing stones observable in the top of F.21 could suggest the post here had been removed rather than allowed to rot *in situ*.

F.18 and 28 were defined as concentrated oval spreads of small to medium-sized stones, in the case of the latter apparently surrounding a soil core. The tops of these features were exposed, but not further excavated.

With the exception of those belonging to the rectangular structure, it is difficult to determine any structural patterning within the excavated post-holes. Similar in size and construction, F.26 and 27 could be regarded as a pair, but seem too closely set to be part of the same structure, with a gap of less than a metre between each of the posts. F.17, 18 and 30 might have formed one side of a square or rectangular building which extends outside the excavated area to the north. Alternatively, they could have acted as entrance posts for a circular building, though this would need to be quite deeply terraced into

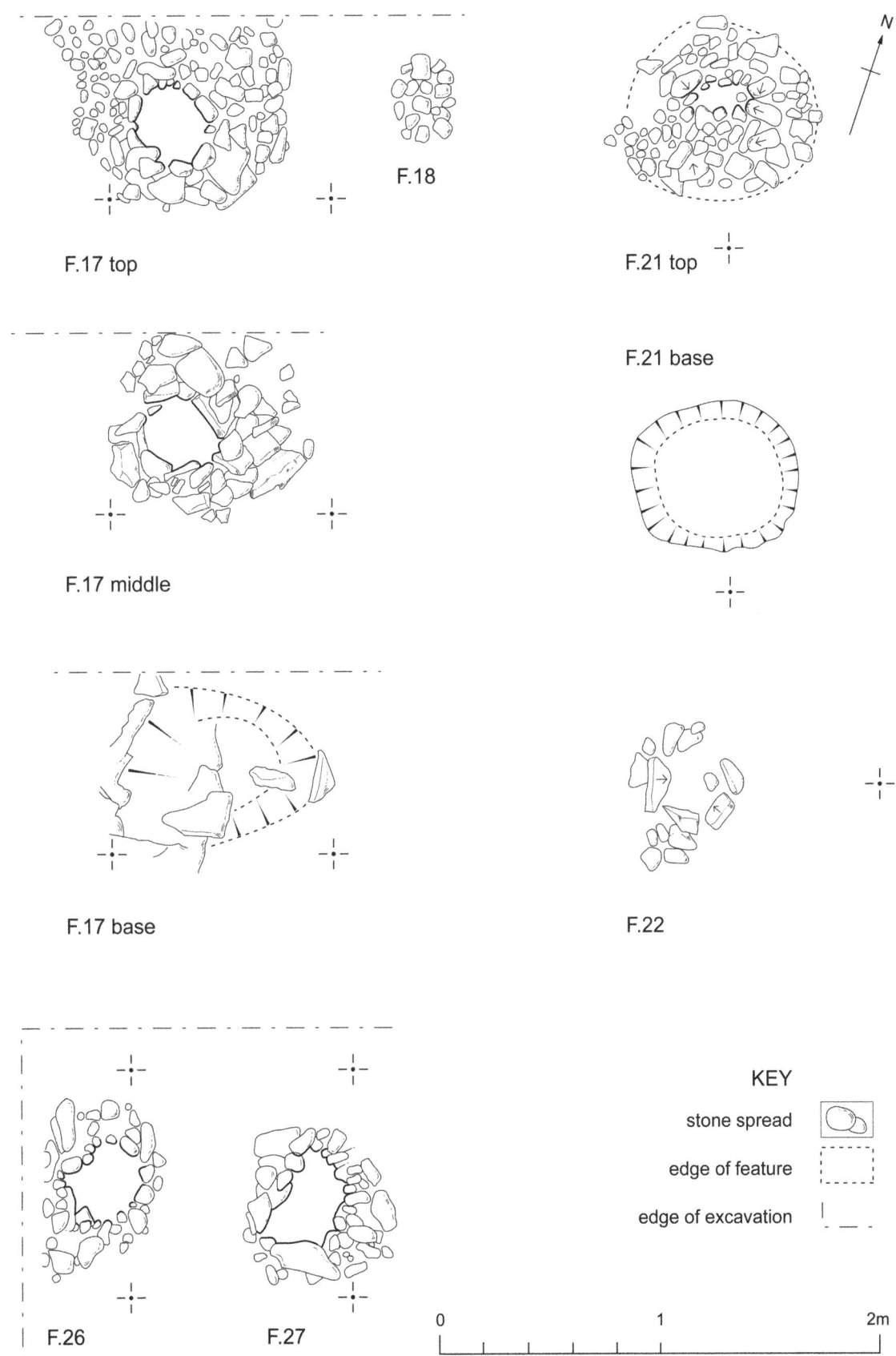

Figure 13. Trench 1. Phase 2 post-holes F.17, 18, 21, 22, 26 and 27

Figure 14. Trench 1. Base of post-hole F.17, from the north

Figure 15. Trench 1. Post-hole F.27 from the north

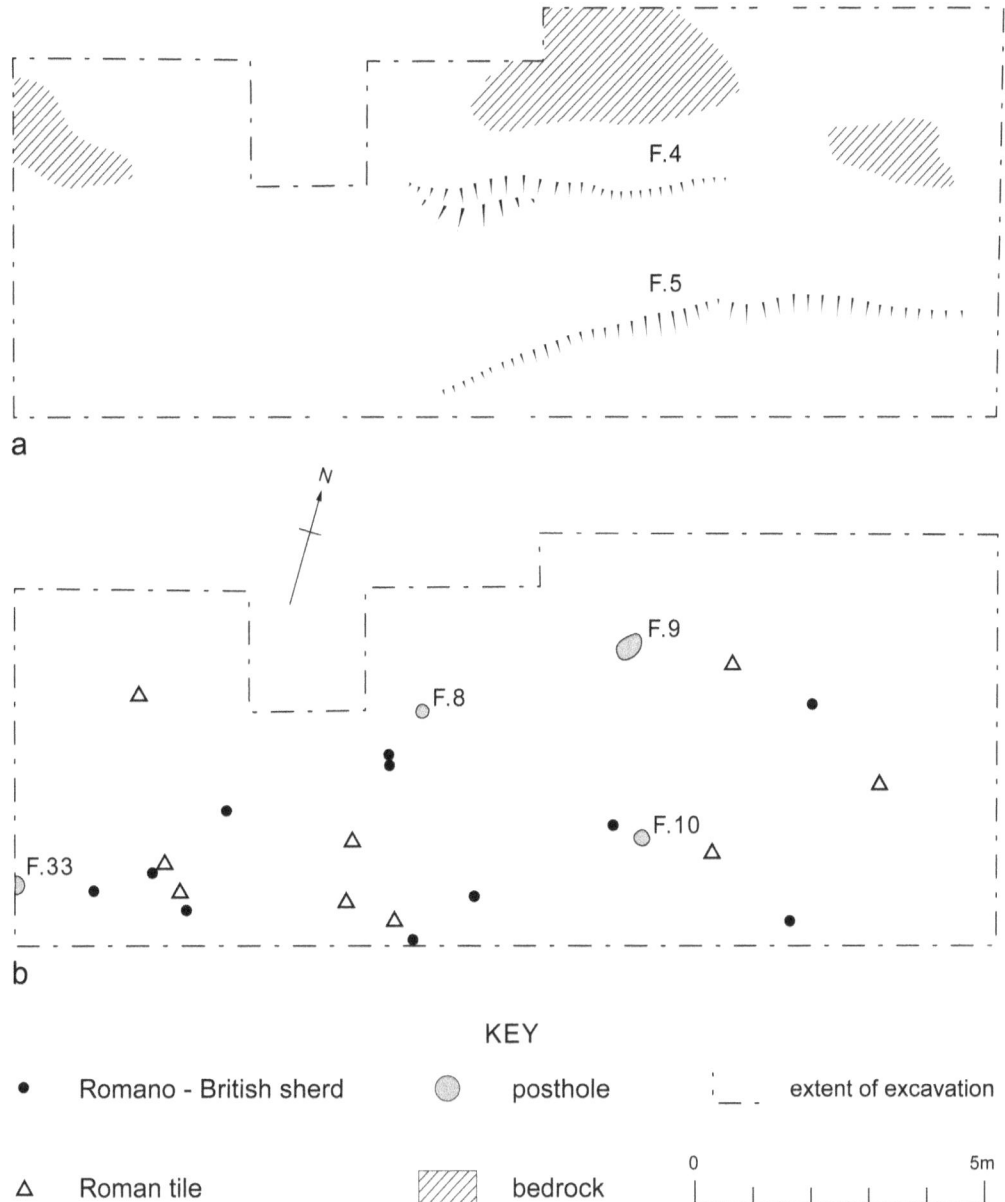

FIGURE 16. TRENCH 1. PHASE 3 (TOP) AND PHASE 4 (BOTTOM) FEATURES

the slope of the ridge behind. Otherwise little pattern is evident. In part this is a product of the limited area of the interior excavation, but also results from the difficulty in identifying all cut features. The pattern may be incomplete. Because of the extensive reworking of the soil, any post-holes that were small or without packing would not be identifiable within the soil layers that filled the quarry hollow and rock-cut scoops.

Phase 3: terraces
Subsequent to the main phase of occupation, two shallow terraces were created across this area of the interior (Figs 16 top & 17). F.4 (top of slope) and F.5 (below) followed the contours of the slope closely, running in a north-east to south-westerly axis across the trench. The southern edge of F.5 was followed over a distance of 10m across the central and eastern section of the trench, whereas F.4 was exposed across its full length. The moderately-angled down-slope edges of F.4 and 5 were sinuous, that of F.4 incorporating three sections of remnant outcropping rock. Their widths ranged from 2-4m, being narrowest over the eastern half of the trench.

The make-up of F.4. [008] comprised a coarse sandstone 'gravel' within a purple-brown clay loam. F.5 made use of the earlier putative up-cast bank formed by [017] (see above); the soil forming the surface of the terrace and the level area below [018] comprising a purple-brown clay loam with occasional sandstone pieces.

FIGURE 17. TRENCH 1. PHASE 3 TERRACES F.4 AND 5, FROM THE SOUTH

With the exception of a single sherd from [018], and a few fragments of fired clay, no material culture was recovered from deposits of this phase. The terraces seem too narrow to have acted as building platforms, and structural evidence is absent from them anyway. It is more likely that they had an agricultural function, perhaps as cultivation terraces.

Phase 4: Roman and later activity
The phase 3 terraces were covered by a deposit of pinkish orange-brown silty clay [002]. This soil was very loose in the upper profile, firmer and more stony towards its base, and became progressively thicker (up to 0.35m) towards the southern edge of the trench. Extensively root disturbed, it contained a low-density spread of Roman pottery and tile, along with two sherds of late Iron Age pottery, 12 pieces of briquetage, an iron loop-headed spike and a late 19th century clay pipe bowl (Fig. 16, bottom).

Four post-holes (F.8, 9, 10 and 33) were recognised to cut through the soil. They ranged in diameter from 0.2m (F.8 and 33) to 0.4m (F.9), with a maximum depth of 0.25m. Discrete cuts were again absent, each feature being defined by steeply pitched and vertical stone packing around a central soil core. Given their dimensions, none of the post-holes would have held substantial timbers. Widely distributed across the excavated area, the post-holes initially make little structural sense. However, allowing for the possibility that one post-hole may have been missed (or was not visible) close to the central southern edge of the trench, F.8-10 could describe three of four corners of a structure approximately 3m square. They clearly belong late in the sequence of activity within this area of the site, and are perhaps tentatively to be associated with the spread of late Iron Age and Roman pottery.

The latest feature was a large, irregular oval hollow, F.2, situated in the south-west corner of the trench. Over 2m across in maximum extent and 0.3m deep, the hollow probably formed as a result of tree-throw. It was filled with a humic dark brown loam [003], very similar in composition to the overlying topsoil [001].

2.3. Trench 2: the inner ditch and bank
The trench location was selected to have the minimum possible impact upon the root systems of standing trees, and an area 21m long and 2m wide was laid out (Figs 18 & 19).

The northern, inner bank (F.1)
Due to time and staffing restrictions, it was not possible to ascertain fully the sequence of activities that produced bank F.1. Although it was hoped to excavate a 2m wide

FIGURE 18. TRENCH 2 UNDER EXCAVATION

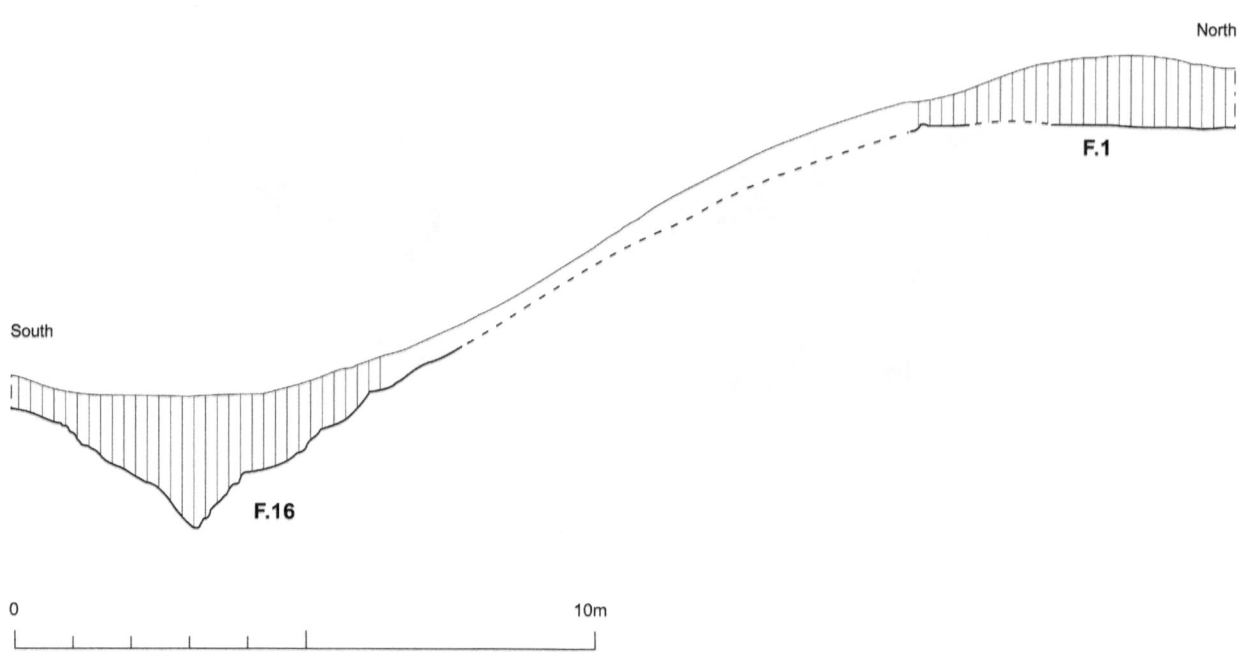

FIGURE 19. TRENCH 2. PROFILE OF INNER BANK (F.1) AND DITCH (F.16)

FIGURE 20. TRENCH 2. BANK UNDER EXCAVATION

section of the bank, in the event it was only possible to dig a 1m wide sondage through all the bank deposits (Fig. 20). Nevertheless, enough was recorded to suggest a long and complex sequence of constructional and possible remodelling events. Although no firm reconstruction of the ramparts was possible, there was enough evidence to suggest that it was formed primarily of loose rubble-walled 'compartments', filled in with earth and further rubble. These were supported by timber lacing, primarily of vertical posts, but perhaps with some additional horizontal elements too.

The bank F.1 was approximately 5.50m wide when excavated, although its full northern extent lay outside Trench 2. It survived to a height of 1.10m, and appeared to have been constructed directly on the undisturbed natural subsoil, a reddish-brown clayey marl (Figs 21 & 22). However, it was not conclusively shown to be natural subsoil, and it is possible that this was an old ground surface, although no trace of a buried soil survived under the bank. It may be that the ground was prepared in some way prior to construction, by being scraped clean of vegetation, levelled and perhaps even deliberately compacted.

Towards the northern extent of Trench 2, deposit [084] was composed of large, tabular sandstone blocks in a pink clay matrix. It was at least 1.30m wide in section, although its full extent lay outside of the trench. This was a very compact layer, and the stones had been laid in a series of horizontal but interlocking layers, forming a very tenacious structure. This was clearly a bank core. However, the southern edge of deposit [084] was quite steep, approximately 60°, and this may indicate that it had been truncated. If so, then this deposit may represent an earlier phase of bank construction.

Towards the southern, outer face of the bank, there were some indications of a possible foundation or bedding cut [110], approximately 1.10-1.20m wide and running east-west along the edge of the natural slope. It was not possible to excavate this feature however. Cut [110] may have formed a secure footing for the stone layer/structure [079]. This consisted of large, tabular sandstone blocks, with a loose matrix of dark reddish-brown silty loam. It may also have been linked to layer/structure [074], a possible revetment or retaining wall. Both of these rubble deposits appeared to have been capped with more clayey material ([066] and [090]). This part of the bank was difficult to elucidate, as it was clear that it had been badly disturbed by erosion.

Rubble deposit [085] may also have been another stone compartment, and may have slumped southwards under pressure into softer earth material. This earth, deposit [092], was a grey silty loam with frequent small sandstone fragments. Deposit [091] was a brownish-red silty loam, with degraded sandstone fragments, but frequent pea grit and charcoal. These seemed to represent earth dumps within the rubble-walled compartments, and the earth was derived from different sources. These deposits may have been supported by timber structures. Cut [087] was the base of an irregular post-hole, 0.23m deep and up to 0.45m wide, and cut into the natural subsoil. It was only seen in plan following the removal of most of the bank material, and was not visible in the drawn section of the bank. However, a concentration of stones was noted in the upper rubble deposit [024], and when the plans were overlaid this was seen to correspond to the position of the post-hole. This suggests that the bank material was built up around a standing vertical timber.

In section, further possible post structures were visible as vertical concentrations of stone, perhaps packing around upright timbers. The soil matrix in these areas was also darker. The putative post-holes [107], [105], [109] and [103] were thus more likely to represent the vertical interface left by posts being removed or rotting *in situ*, rather than intrusive posthole cuts. Again, this suggests that stone compartments and rubble dumps were built up around timber structures. These post interfaces might also have marked different constructional episodes, for they were associated with a complex series of further stone rubble and earth dumps. Post interface [103] was rather high up in the sequence, and may have represented a later remodelling phase.

Layer [030] may have been another stone structure within the bank, and two sherds of Iron Age pottery were recovered from within it. It was associated with a series of earth and rubble dumps, layers [082], [080], [111], [112], [058], [068] and [067]. Burnt bone was recovered from deposit [082], and two fragments of Droitwich briquetage from [080]. These deposits seemed to have been closely associated with post interfaces [107], [105] and [109], and were probably reinforced by them.

Deposits [024] and [005] were general layers of mixed and eroded material below the topsoil, which overlay all other bank deposits. Deposit [024] in particular contained many large, tabular sandstone blocks, and was likely originally to have formed part of a substantial stone structure. The stone packing in post interfaces [107], [105] and [103] clearly protruded into this deposit, indicating that these posts would have been supporting such a stone structure. This may well have formed the most substantial part of the ramparts, such as a stone facing and/or walkway, and it is likely that most of the stone rubble in the ditch deposits was originally derived from this structure.

Post interface [109] did not appear to protrude into deposit [024] however. This may indicate that it was removed or sawn off prior to the deposition of [024]. However, the northernmost extent of [024] may be comprised of erosional material rather than *in situ* bank deposits, and this post may not have been a major structural element. It is possible for example, that it reinforced and stabilised a walkway behind the ramparts.

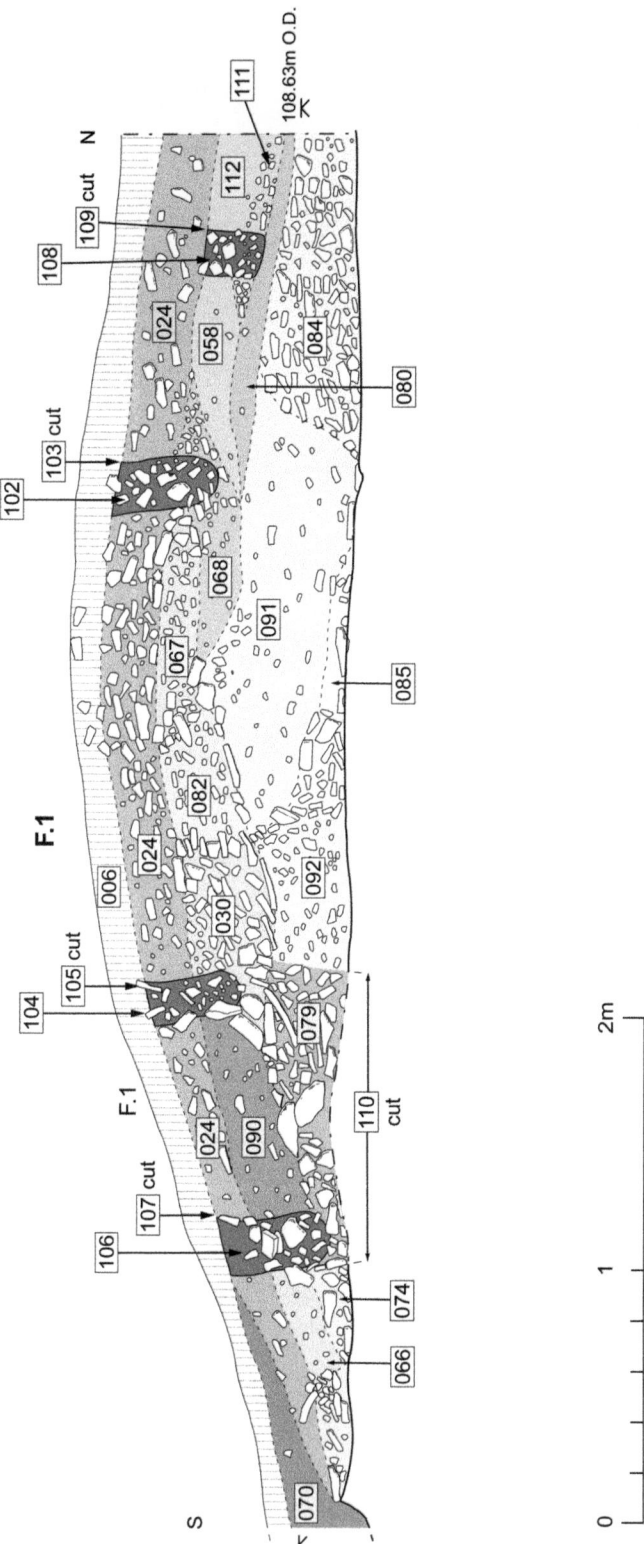

FIGURE 21. TRENCH 2. EAST-FACING SECTION OF BANK

FIGURE 22. TRENCH 2. EAST-FACING BANK SECTION

The southern, outer bank (F.31)
Only the northernmost, inner edge of this southern outer bank was revealed in Trench 2, by deposits [099] and [101], about 0.50m of its width (Fig. 23). These consisted largely of clayey marl and clayey loam, and may have been derived from the up-cast created by the digging of ditch cut [088] (F.16). Some of the deposits in ditch F.16 were derived from erosion off this bank, and were also mostly clayey marl in nature.

The possible revetment (F.15)
This possible structure (deposit [031]) was located south and downslope of bank F.16. Between F.16 and F.15 was a gently sloping gap or 'berm' approximately 1.50m wide, and this may have been artificially terraced into the hillside. Beyond this the natural slope fell away steeply at roughly 60° or more, and it was at this point that between 10-30 courses of medium-sized sandstone blocks had been revetted into the hillside. This revetting was at least 2.00m wide, but tumble downslope [069] from this feature obscured its original extent. The area of the 'berm' and the revetment was also badly disturbed by tree roots.

The ditch (F.16)
The ditch cut [088] (F.16) was a massive affair, and was a maximum of 2.20m deep from the top of the deposits at its central point (Figs 23 & 24). Its sides were smooth and steep to the south, dropping at approximately 60°. To the north, [088] was more irregular, and slightly less steep (c.45°). It clearly made clever use of differences in the underlying natural drift and solid geology. The southern side of the ditch was cut into natural compact red and reddish-brown clayey marl. The latter must have formed glacial drift deposits against the side of the hill. The northern side of the ditch by contrast, was cut into the natural, red sandstone solid geology. The ditch therefore largely followed the marl-sandstone interface. The natural bedding planes of the red sandstone caused the irregular, stepped appearance of the northern ditch edge. These bedding planes dipped southwards at approximately 20°.

The northern and southern limits of the cut edge could not be located precisely. To the south, it was not clear from the section where ditch F.16 ended, and where the southern bank F.31 began. To the north, the ditch cut graded into the natural steep slope of the hill. The builders of the hillfort defences were clearly making use of a very steep pre-existing natural slope. The bottom of cut [088] (and the possible re-cut) consisted of a narrow and concave spade-dug slot, perhaps meant as a defensive 'ankle-breaker' feature. This may be merely the product of spade digging, however.

Primary deposition in the ditch consisted of the compact reddish-brown clayey marl [076], which contained some sandstone fragments. This deposit was partially derived from re-deposited natural marl, the majority of this probably coming from the southern edge of the ditch. It contained some flecks of charcoal, and also a lump of possible carbonised wood.

A series of stratigraphically later deposits formed above [076], and consisted of silt and slump episodes. The interface between these deposits and [076], together with

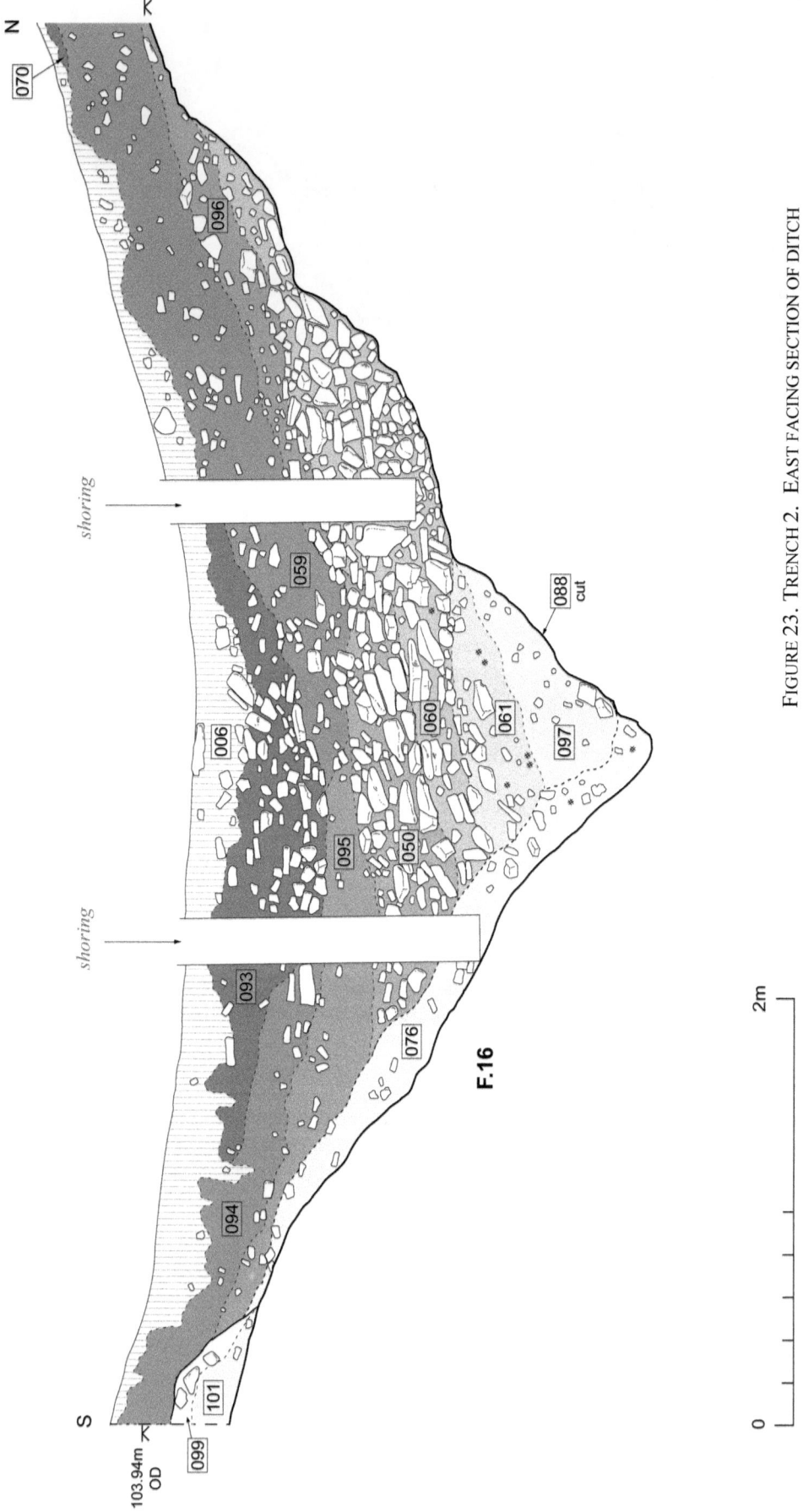

FIGURE 23. TRENCH 2. EAST FACING SECTION OF DITCH

FIGURE 24. TRENCH 2. EAST-FACING DITCH SECTION.
NOTE THAT THE STEPS ON THE LEFT-HAND SIDE ARE A PRODUCT OF EXCAVATION

an apparent 'step' in the cut profile, suggested that there could have been at least one re-cutting episode. This was not clear enough to number as a distinct cut interface however. Deposit [097] was a compact, dark reddish-brown clayey marl with dark mottles caused by manganese flecking. It contained some angular sandstone fragments, but no charcoal or finds. It may have been partially derived from the slumping off the northern bank.

Deposit [061] was either the last of the primary ditch deposits, or the first of a series of slumping deposits. It consisted of a brick red clayey marl with some large and angular sandstone fragments, and some lenses of greenish-grey clay. Like [097] it was probably partially derived from slumping from the north. It contained charcoal flecks and lumps of unidentifiable carbonised material. It also contained burnt bone and numerous sherds of Iron Age pottery from a single vessel.

Deposits [060] and [050] consisted of loose, large and angular sandstone fragments, in a matrix of friable reddish-brown clayey loam. From the tip lines in the rubble fills, it was clear that most of the sandstone fragments were derived from the north or upslope side of the trench. Three sherds of Roman pottery (including a piece of decorated samian), several fragments of tile and a sandstone rubber were recovered from deposit [060].

Following these slumping episodes, further deposits built up that were a mixture of material eroding off both banks, including more sandstone rubble from the inner bank, and silts forming in the hollow of the ditch. These interdigitating deposits consisted of clayey loams, and included [095], [059], [094], and [093]. A fragment of Romano-British tile was recovered from deposit [059].

The lower interface of topsoil [006] was very irregular in the concave depression formed by the ditch deposits. This indicated considerable root and earthworm activity, no doubt due to the relatively damp nature of the soils in the ditch.

2.4. Trench 3: the western entrance

The western entrance was investigated by means of a single 10.25 x 3.00m trench, orientated east-west, and positioned over the northern half of the inner entrance and the northern terminal of the inner bank (F.29). The extent of the excavated area was restricted by vegetation cover, and by the need to retain access along a footpath running through the entrance. Prior to excavation, the entrance was clearly visible as a 7m wide 'cut' following a straight course through the inner rampart. On both sides, the inner bank survived to a height of around 2m. The bank terminals were expanded as they abutted the entrance, much more so on the south than the north. That on the south attains a width of up to 8.7m, forming a relatively level platform on top of which is a smaller raised area that follows the inner edge of the bank for a distance of c.12m (Coxe's 'tumulus').

Excavation revealed a complex sequence of deposits relating to an original entrance, perhaps three phases of

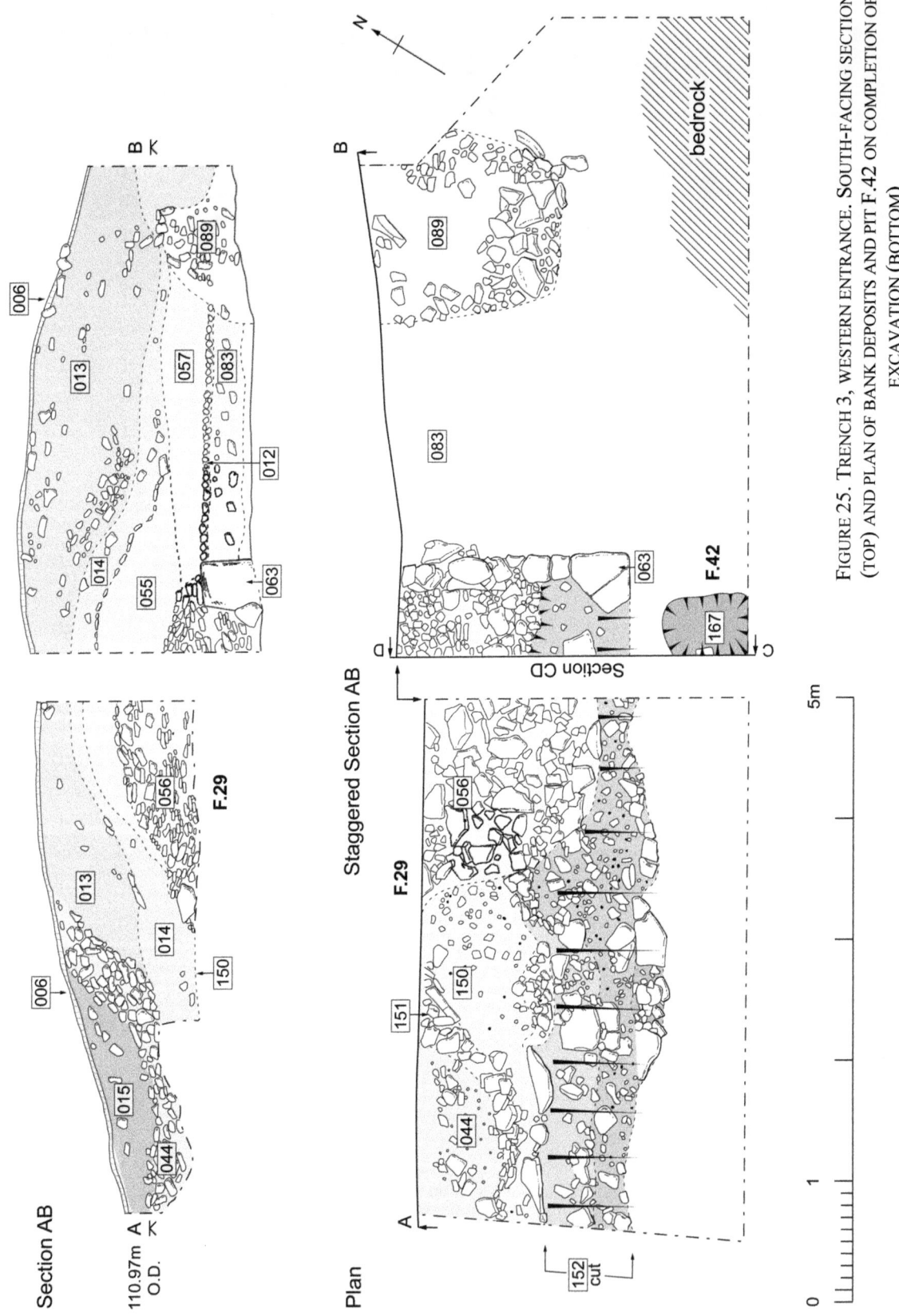

FIGURE 25. TRENCH 3, WESTERN ENTRANCE. SOUTH-FACING SECTION (TOP) AND PLAN OF BANK DEPOSITS AND PIT F.42 ON COMPLETION OF EXCAVATION (BOTTOM)

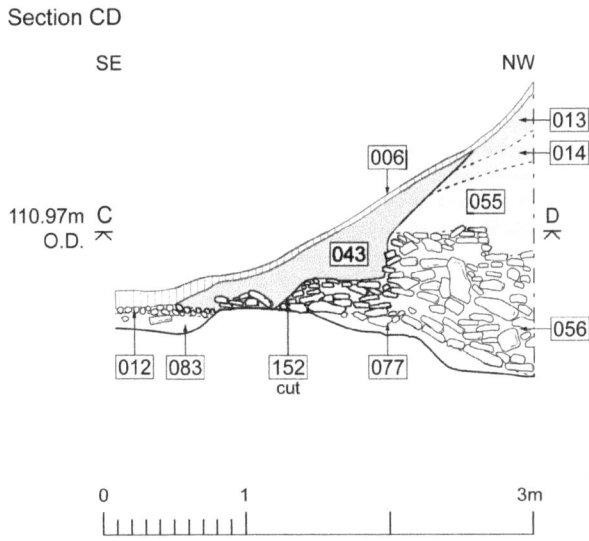

FIGURE 26. TRENCH 3. SECTION CD SHOWING BANK DEPOSITS AND LATER RE-CUT OF ENTRANCE (CUT [152])

bank construction and a later re-definition of the entrance (Figs 25 & 26). Over the eastern half of the trench these deposits were subject to extensive excavation, with most areas being taken down to the sandstone natural. Investigation in the western half was, however, largely limited to the excavation of later deposits.

The first phase stone bank and entrance
The sequence begins with the construction of a low stone-revetted bank incorporating a recessed area or 'guard chamber' at the rear (Fig. 27). The surface of the geological natural here was uneven, particularly towards the eastern end of the trench where a 0.3m deep depression observed to run beyond the north section was filled with a loose grey-brown silty clay [083] containing angular sandstone rubble and frequent charcoal flecks. Abutting part of the first phase bank, this episode of levelling is closely tied to the construction of the defences. Reflecting the tilted bedding of the geology across the area, a corresponding outcrop of sandstone projected through the surface in the south-east corner of the trench. The first phase bank comprised a low (maximum height 1.2m) and wide (9m+) stone structure. It was discontinuous across its width within the excavated area, with a 2.0-2.2m wide and 2+m deep recess towards the rear (the back wall of this feature was not exposed in the excavation.). Forming what would traditionally be described as a 'guard chamber', the primary function of this feature need not, however, be related to defence (see discussion below).

The bank possessed a cellular structure, being constructed as a series of bays containing dumps of sandstone rubble. On the eastern side of the chamber the bank was composed of large angular sandstone rubble within a grey-brown silty clay [089]. Perhaps originally revetted by timber, this deposit formed a well-defined mass of material up to 1.6m wide, with gently curving sides and a squared terminal set slightly back from the line of the passageway to the west of the chamber (i.e. indicating that the mouth of the entrance opened out into the interior). On the western side there was a regularly constructed stone revetment wall [063], originally continued along the north side of the entrance passage. The face of the walling had been 'robbed-out' along most of the passage length during a later phase when the entrance was re-established. Here the walling could be seen to be up to 0.8m thick, perhaps originally slightly battered back and with a core of small to medium sandstone blocks. However, on the western side of the 'guard chamber' it survived well, being made-up of medium to large (0.2-0.5m) tabular sandstone blocks set in a regular coursed wall up to 0.4m high, highest on the north side where it dipped into the natural hollow. This acted as a retaining wall for a series of cells and dump deposits making up the body of the bank. At its core was a discrete mass of angular sandstone rubble [056]/[064], loosely packed with numerous hollows and lenses of dark grey-brown silty clay. Up to 2.2m across and 1.2m deep, this deposit had a well defined though sloping edge on the west side and abutted [063] on the east and south. Though much of the stone lay horizontal or at a shallow angle, several blocks were steeply pitched or set upright. The latter occurred around two loose patches within the rubble, both c.0.2-0.3m in diameter and set 0.8m apart, close to the section edge. Though not confirmed during excavation, these may well represent post settings for a projecting timber rampart, palisade, or even a gate structure.

Dumped against [053]/[064] was a thick deposit of sandstone rubble within a reddish silty clay [150]. On the west this abutted a length of irregular curving stone wall [151] forming a cell 1.9+ x 0.9+m across and filled with a similar rubble matrix to [150]. Located at the front of the rampart, this appears to have formed a projecting hornwork. The upper components of [150] and [151] were both exposed but only partially excavated.

Within the entranceway itself was a sub-rectangular pit or scoop (F.42, [167]), 0.75+ x 0.50+m across and 0.20m deep, with shallow sloping sides and a flat base. Filled with a loose grey-brown silty clay containing sandstone pieces [153], the status of this feature is uncertain. Its regularity suggests it is artificial rather than natural, and it may represent a shallow post-hole forming part of a gate structure. However, it was sealed by a cobble surface, [012], which extended across the whole of the entrance area. The latter was made-up of a thin (up to 0.1m) but closely set and compact layer of rounded sandstone cobbles (perhaps collected from the nearby River Usk) within a clay matrix. Wear was only present on this surface in the centre of the passageway where it had been exposed during the later re-establishment of the entrance. In fact, one of the remarkable features of the original entranceway was the absence of any evident weathering

FIGURE 27. TRENCH 3. EAST END OF ENTRANCE ON COMPLETION OF EXCAVATION, SHOWING AREA OF 'GUARD CHAMBER'

or the kinds of erosion normally associated with human, animal or vehicular traffic. Nor were any finds recovered from contexts associated with it. This implies that the entrance was little used and probably very short-lived.

The second phase bank, entrance blocking and collapse deposits

After an unknown interval the bank was considerably heightened, the 'guard chamber' infilled and the entrance blocked. A series of clay and stone dumps took the bank to a maximum up-standing height of over 2m. The sequence begins with deposit [057], a loose mottled orange-brown friable clay containing angular sandstone rubble and flecks of charcoal, between 0.2-0.4m thick, which was used to level the chamber area. This was in turn covered by a similar though more compact matrix of material [055], up to 0.7m thick and spread over a width of 3.4m within the centre of the bank. [032], a thin layer of sandstone blocks and smaller sub-angular and angular sandstone pieces within a reddish clay, capped [055] on its eastern side. This was followed by a lens of red clay with greenish, decayed, marl pea-grit [025], restricted to the eastern side of the bank, and more substantial deposits of mixed reddish-purple clay containing small sandstone fragments, [014] and [013]. Both [014] and [013] extended across nearly the full width of the bank, the former being more compact and thicker towards the western side. In each instance, the presumed source of this material must be an accompanying ditch or the partially silted internal quarry pits. Some tip-lines were noted within [013] following the profile of the bank, always on the basis of variations in stone density. More apparent in section than in plan, it was not possible to isolate separate tips or dumps of material within individual contexts during excavation. Although searched for, no signs of timber-lacing or revetting were observed.

Capping the front (western side) of the enlarged bank was a thick (0.2-0.4m) deposit of large and fresh sandstone rubble [044]. Extending to the foot of the bank, its upper profile was truncated and it cannot therefore be said whether it extended to the top of that feature. This deposit was without obvious structure. While it might have been intentionally created to form a rubble face or façade to the bank, it could equally represent material from a stone superstructure that had collapsed or had been deliberately slighted. Certainly the truncation of the upper profiles of [044] and [013] suggest that the top of the bank was levelled at some late stage.

Overlying [044] was a dense but loosely structured deposit of medium-sized rubble within a reddish-purple silty clay [015]. Up to 0.4m thick, this was restricted to the front of the bank. While perhaps a later stone capping, it might, more economically, be interpreted as representing further collapse of a bank-top stone wall or rampart. Over the eastern (inner) slope of the bank was a thin scatter of medium-sized sandstone blocks [016] extending over an area of 4.0 x 1.2m. This may again represent a decay/weathering deposit.

28

Late re-definition of the entrance
At a later date the infilled entrance was reinstated. A passage was cut through the second phase dump rampart, in the process also truncating the stone revetment of the first phase bank. The cut [152] extended across the full width of the bank and was deep enough to expose in its centre the earlier cobbled surface [012]. From surface indications alone, this later entrance was in the order of 7m wide at the top and perhaps 4m at its base. The cut has a stepped profile where it was worked into the stonework of the first phase bank, creating a ledge c.0.3-0.5m wide running along the northern side of the re-defined entrance passage. It is possible that the 'knoll' on the south bank flanking the entrance (Coxe's 'tumulus') was created through the dumping of spoil from this construction work.

A thin reddish-brown clay loam with small sandstone inclusions [019] formed against the edge of the entrance passage. This in turn was overlain by a weathering deposit [043], comprising a compact pink clay with fragments of greenish decayed marl and sandstone gravel, restricted to the sides of the cut. There were no indications of any formal revetment to the reinstated entrance, nor a gate structure, though the step created alongside the passageway could have acted as a base for a timber revetment set into a sill-beam.

The only artefacts recovered from the entrance area were a small piece of brick and a sherd of modern glass from the exposed surface of [012].

3. Artefactual Material

Quantities of pottery, briquetage (salt container), ceramic building material, ironwork and worked stone were recovered during the excavation; the bulk of this material coming from deposits within Trench 1. The distribution of these finds according to trench, phase and context is given in Table 2.

	Iron Age Pottery	Briquetage	Fired clay	Iron object	Worked flint	Worked stone	Roman pottery	Tile
TRENCH 1								
Phase 1								
[010], F.25	4 (3)	-	-	Fitting?	-	2 discs	-	-
[011], F.23	16+ (55)	3 (20)	7 (25)	Joiner's dog	-	Pounder, rubber	-	-
[028], F.24	-	-	2 (2)	-	-	-	-	-
[037], F.23	7 (19)	-	3+ (4)	-	-	-	-	-
[038], F.24	2 (29)	-		-	-	-	-	-
[042], F.23	3 (16)	3 (32)	2 (4)	-	-	-	-	-
[048]	-	4 (3)	-	-	-	-	-	-
Sub-total	*32+ (122)*	*10 (55)*	*14+ (35)*	-	-	*4*	-	-
Phase 2								
[017]	-	-	1 (1)	-	1	-	-	-
[027], F.3	12 (64)	2 (18)	1 (3)	Brooch	-	-	-	-
[033]	2 (3)	-	3 (3)	-	-	-	-	-
Sub-total	*14 (67)*	*2 (18)*	*5 (7)*	-	*1*	-	-	-
Phase 3								
[008], F.4	-	-	1 (2)	-	-	-	-	-
[018]	1 (2)	-	17+ (11)	-	-	-	-	-
Sub-total	*1 (2)*	-	*18+ (13)*	-	-	-	-	-
Phase 4								
[002]	2 (34)	12 (62)	26+ (58)	Spike	1	2 grooved blocks, pounder	14	10
[001]					-	Pounder		
Sub-total	*2 (34)*	*12 (62)*	*26+ (58)*	-	*1*	*4*	*14*	*10*
TRENCH 2								
[030], F.1	2 (7)	-	-	-	-	-	-	-
[080], F.1	-	2 (26)	-	-	-	-	-	-
[060], F.16	-	-	-	-	-	Rubber	3	14
[061], F.16	32 (60)	-	-	-	-	-	-	-
Sub-total	*34 (67)*	*2 (26)*	-	-	-	*1*	*3*	*14*
TRENCH 3								
[012]	-	-	-	-	-	-	-	1
[055]	-	-	4 (8g)	-	-	-	-	-

TABLE 2. SUMMARY OF FINDS ACCORDING TO CONTEXT

3.1. Ironwork
Philip Macdonald

1. Loop-headed spike (Trench 1, [002], Find no.187)
Rectangular-sectioned stem, which thickens in the middle and tapers towards a point at one end and narrows towards a small loop at the other (Fig. 28.1). Only part of the loop survives. Length 133mm, external diameter of ring (estimated) 15-20mm.

Loop-headed spikes were used to provide a ring which could be attached to woodwork or masonry. Such rings could have served a multitude of purposes (cf. Manning 1985, 129-30).

2. Possible hemispherical fitting (Trench 1, [010], Find no.185)
Hollow hemispherical fitting filled with mineralised organic material. Investigative cleaning suggests that the organic material is derived from the burial environment (P.Parkes pers. comm.). Corrosion has removed the original surface of the object. Function uncertain, possibly a fragment of a dome-headed stud. Diameter 20-21mm, height 15mm.

3. Possible Joiner's dog (Trench 1, [011], Find no.184)
Tapering, rectangular-sectioned, L-shaped rod, broken at both ends (Fig. 28.2). Possibly the arm and part of the adjoining section of a small joiner's dog. Surviving length 16mm, surviving depth of arm 31mm.

Joiner' dogs are a form of staple used for joining two pieces of timber (cf. Manning 1985, 131). Comparable, Iron Age examples of the type are known from Balksbury Camp, Hampshire (Wainwright & Davies 1995, 39, nos. 19 & 21, fig. 42) and Danebury, Hampshire (Cunliffe & Poole 1991, 353, no. 2334, fig. 7.24).

4. La Tène I brooch (Trench 1, F.3, [027], Find no.186)
La Tène I type brooch with a plano-convex sectioned, arched bow, oval-sectioned pin and eight-coiled spring mechanism with an external chord and iron axial rod (Fig. 28.3). The top of the bow is decorated with a set of transverse ridges defined by three evenly spaced grooves which only extend around the front half of the bow. The foot of the brooch is missing. Surviving length 49mm, width of bow-head 20.5mm, transverse diameter of the spring coils 7.5mm.

Although the brooch appears to have a true bilateral spring consisting of eight coils and an external chord, it actually has a mock-spring mechanism. Mock-springs are not unusual features on La Tène I brooches. With a mock-spring mechanism the brooch's pin is connected to only one of the coils which turns like a hinge. The remainder of the 'spring' mechanism is non-functional but gives the impression that the brooch has a complete spring. With this arrangement the tension provided by a true spring is lost and so to stiffen the hinge mechanism of the pin it is necessary to insert an axial rod through the coils and bow-head of the brooch (for a discussion of mock-spring mechanisms cf. Hodson 1971, 54-6; Hull & Hawkes 1987, 2, 74). La Tène I brooches with eight coils are rare but not unknown in British contexts; copper alloy examples are recorded from Burton Fleming, East Yorkshire (Stead 1979, 94, fig. 36.1; Stead 1991, 81, 219, no. A1, fig. 120) and Ravensburgh Castle, Hertfordshire (Dyer 1976, 157, fig. 3; Hull & Hawkes 1987, 103, no. 6932, pl. 30). It is notable that both the Burton Fleming and Ravensburgh Castle examples also have mock-spring mechanisms.

Despite the main defining feature of the reverted foot being missing, the form of the bow and the absence of evidence for the foot having been attached to the bow indicates that the brooch is a La Tène I type. The relatively small transverse diameter of the spring's coils suggests that the brooch is an example of the La Tène 1B type (Hull & Hawkes 1987, 87-115). It is not possible typologically to subdivide the brooch any further with confidence, although it is probably an example of Hull and Hawkes' Type 1Ba or 1Bb (1987, 95-106). The vogue of Type 1B La Tène brooches mainly dates to the first half of the 4th century BC, although there are some later survivals (Hull & Hawkes 1987, 97; Haselgrove 1997, fig. 8.1).

Although the majority of known examples of La Tène brooches are cast from copper alloy this does not necessarily indicate that examples forged from iron were unusual during antiquity. The bias in favour of copper alloy brooches is probably a result of their preferential survival and retrieval over iron examples. This point is illustrated by the results of recent excavations, such as those in East Yorkshire (Stead 1991, 80) and Castell Henllys, Pembrokeshire (A. Gwilt pers. comm.), where the majority of recovered brooches were of iron.

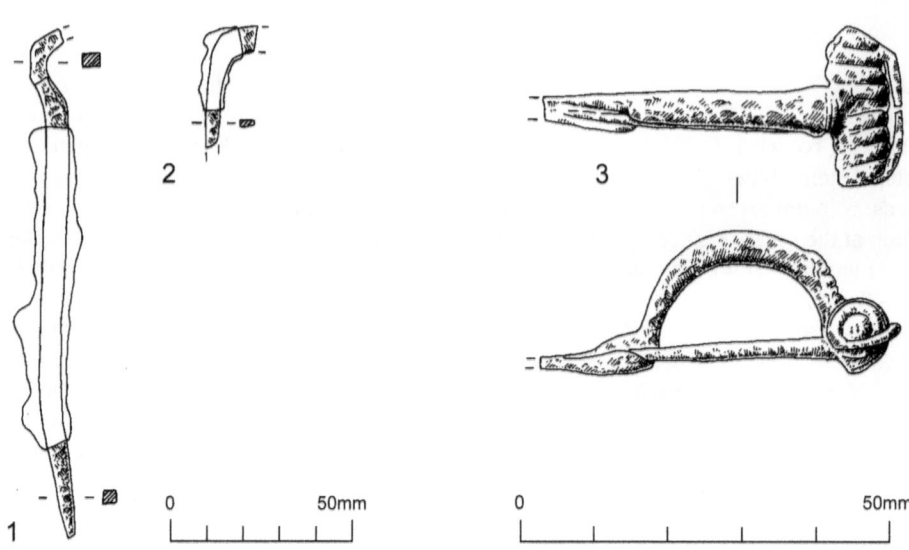

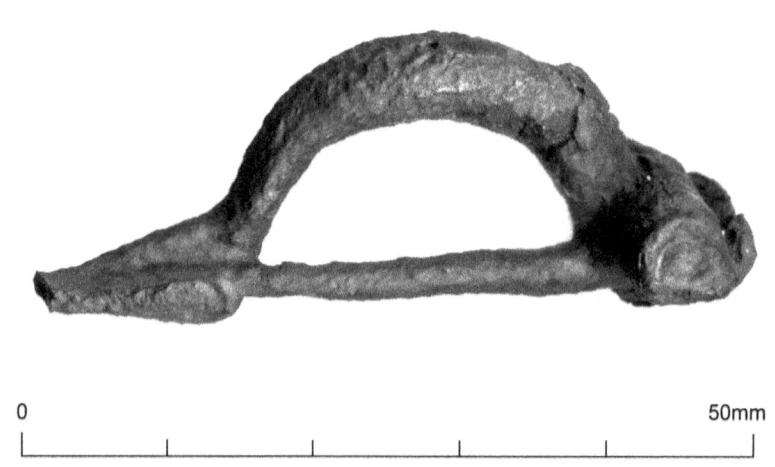

FIGURE 28. METALWORK: 1, LOOP-HEADED SPIKE (TRENCH 1, [002]); 2. POSSIBLE JOINER'S DOG (TRENCH 1, [011]); 3. LA TÈNE I BROOCH (TRENCH 1, F.3, [027])

3.2. Metalworking slags
T.P. Young

This small assemblage of slag comprises three pieces which are certainly blacksmithing slags and one piece which is probably so. All of the slags show evidence for the use of charcoal as fuel. Such slags are not indicative of age, with charcoal-fuelled blacksmithing in clay-lined hearths being the dominant smithing process until the industrial period. The small size of the assemblage and the relatively large size of the slag pieces suggests that the smithing was taking place elsewhere on the site.

Description

1. [010] adjacent to F.26

Medium-sized plano-convex slag cake, weighing 475g and measuring 105 x 80 x 53mm deep. The upper surface shows an irregular surface, but with a smooth zone proximally. The lower surface is irregular proximally, with accreted grains derived from hearth wall. Distally the lower surface is smoother, with impressions of fine organic remains, suggestive of original fire kindling. There is no well-developed proximal burr (attachment area to hearth wall below blowhole), but a small, attached lump of wall and the location of the smooth patch on the upper surface suggests that the cake may have grown somewhat obliquely to the wall.

The slag cake has been sectioned along its long axis. The section reveals a very porous internal structure, with voids created by charcoal inclusions. The only dense, non-vesicular, slags form a thin (up to 5mm) layer extending out from below the smooth zone on the upper surface.

2. [028], F.11
Four pieces of material, two of which are natural stones.

The smaller piece of slag is of a sheet-like form, rectangular, 45 x 55mm and up to 15mm thick and weighs 70g. One of the long sides shows a fracture surface and is of a twisted appearance. This might imply that this is the side of attachment to the furnace wall, or that the piece has broken off from a larger slag block when still hot and plastic. The upper surface is smooth but irregularly and finely lobate, with some impressed charcoal. The lower surface is more coarsely lobate, with charcoal impressions and some charcoal.

The larger slag piece is a D-shaped piece of slag cake, 105 x 85mm wide and 40mm deep, weighing 385g. The straight side represents a fracture, and is approximately 80mm long. The cake is concavo-convex, having a raised outer lip around the upper surface. The upper surface bears impressions and fragments of rather fine charcoal (up to 15mm). The lower surface is mainly coated in adhering sediment/lining, but shows some fine elongate organic material, probably the kindling. The piece was sectioned approximately along its proximal-distal axis. The section shows a uniform highly vesicular slag with abundant inclusions of charcoal.

3. [038]
Small slag cake with an almost hemispherical shape, 70 x 65mm and 35mm deep, weighing 185g. The upper surface is smooth, with greenish glass superficially at one end, extending over margin of upper surface and 15mm down the side of the cake (proximally?). The lower surface is irregular, but some patches are smoothly and finely lobate around small charcoal impressions. One side shows a 13 x 20mm area of attachment to a piece of sandstone. It is not clear whether this is a small pebble, or a small attachment to a larger piece.

The slag cake has been sectioned along its long axis. The section reveals a two-layer structure, with an upper, largely non-vesicular, layer up to 15mm thick, and a lower layer with vesicles, often elongated in vertical direction, 20mm thick.

Discussion
The assemblage is very small, merely indicating the presence of iron-working in the general area, rather than particularly close to the findspot. All the slags are compatible with blacksmithing. Three of the four are varieties of plano-convex smithing hearth cakes; the fourth is possibly a piece of a small cake. The weights of the three fairly complete cakes (185, 385 and 475g) fall within the range of typical blacksmithing slag cakes (Crew 1996 gave the range of typical smithing cakes as 200-500g within an overall range of 100 to 2000g).

The internal structure of the cakes is generally rather vesicular, with two examples showing evidence for a slightly denser slag pool on top. This may be evidence that the hearths were being employed for general purpose smithing, rather than, for instance, intense prolonged fire welding.

3.3. Prehistoric pottery
Rick Peterson, Joshua Pollard & Elaine Morris

Eighty-three sherds and several crumbs (292g) of prehistoric pottery were recovered during the excavation, the majority (49 sherds: 225g) coming from deposits in the interior of Trench 1, the remainder (34 sherds: 67g) from the bank and ditch in Trench 2 (Fig. 29; Tables 3 & 4). Though forming a small assemblage, the sherds are generally in good condition and all came from stratified contexts.

All sherds were examined macroscopically and under x10-30 magnification in order to facilitate identification of fabrics. Details of fabric colour, hardness and surface finish were noted, along with information on sherd condition and vessel form. Inclusions were identified with reference to the algorithm suggested in Peacock (1977, 30-2). Three fabrics (1, 2 and 3) were subject to petrological examination by Dr Elaine Morris, and both the macroscopic and petrological descriptions are given in these instances. Where possible, sherds have been assigned to specific vessels; although it should be stressed that the vessel numbers (16 in all) represent a minimum count of the number of pots originally present. Note that vessels 6 and 18, originally considered to be Iron Age, have since been assigned Roman and medieval dates respectively.

Detailed descriptions
Fabric Group 1: medium to fine vesicular mudstone (Malvernian Group D; Morris 1982).
A moderately hard fabric with an irregular fracture. The fabric is gritted with plentiful medium to fine fragments of mudstone. This material has decayed leaving large numbers of voids or vesicles in the fabric. The fabric also contained very sparse sub-angular fragments of quartz. Malvernian D (Morris 1982).

Petrological analysis was undertaken on sherds from vessels 14 and 17. These displayed an argillaceous / vesicular fabric with a 40-50% abundant concentration of angular vesicles ($\leq$1.5mm across) which once held loosely-structured mudstones, and a background clay matrix containing a sparse amount of sub-angular quartz measuring $\leq$0.3mm across.

Parts of ten vessels survive from fabric group 1. Vessel 1 appears to be a slack shouldered jar with a simple upright rim, possibly around 120mm in diameter at the rim. Vessels 3, 12 and 17 are represented by single body sherds. Vessel 4 is another single sherd, in this case part of a flat base of around 90mm diameter. A small fragment of a pointed rim survives from vessel 7, along with two small body sherds. A large number of sherds survive from vessel 8, three of which belong to a simple upright rim, around 120mm in diameter. Some sherds of vessel 8 appear to have been hand-wiped. A simple, slightly in-turned rim and a single body sherd from vessel 14 show that this vessel was burnished externally and was around 140mm in diameter at the rim. Vessel 15 was a slack shouldered jar with a simple upright rim and a flat base. It was burnished externally and was around 150mm in diameter at the rim and around 90mm at the base. It is possible that the base sherd recorded as vessel 4 was a part of vessel 15. Vessel 16 is represented by another small base sherd. Sooting is present on sherds from vessels 14 and 15, indicating their use as cooking pots.

Fabric Group 2: coarse crushed quartzite.
A moderately hard fabric with an irregular fracture. It was tempered using plentiful coarse and very coarse angular crushed quartzite fragments, plentiful fine to medium rounded quartzite sand particles and sparse sandstone fragments.

Petrological analysis was undertaken on the sherd from vessel 2. This identified numerous large angular fragments of quartz (≤2mm across) and two pieces of sandstone also <2mm across (possibly a ferruginous cement, but this could be siliceous) in a slightly micaceous, very dense background clay matrix; most likely a tempered fabric.

This fabric was used to make vessel 2, represented by a single, simple rim.

Fabric Group 3: Malvernian Group D variant.
A moderately hard fabric with a laminated fracture, containing moderate amounts of coarse mudstone fragments.

Petrological analysis was undertaken on a sherd from vessel 13. This displayed an iron-rich, very micaceous (nearly quartz-free) clay matrix with a common (20-25%) concentration of angular argillaceous matter which appears to be similar to mudstones and/or vesicles where the stones once existed. It is similar in many ways to Fabric 1, but the frequency of mudstones and the presence of a very micaceous, nearly quartz-free, clay matrix supports a separate definition.

Parts of two vessels survive from fabric group 3. Vessel 5 is a slack shouldered jar with a beaded rim, and appears to have been around 150mm in diameter at the rim. The vessel had been smoothed externally, probably using a bone or wooden spatula. Vessel 13 is a slack shouldered jar with a simple upright rim, in this case around 230mm in diameter. It retains traces of sooting.

Fabric Group 4: Malvernian Group D variant.
A moderately hard fabric with a laminated fracture. This fabric is similar to the vesicular fabric group 1, but also containing coarse rounded clay pellets and sparse coarse rounded sandstone. Six body sherds in fabric group 4 survive from vessels 9 and 10. Probably Malvernian D.

Fabric Group 5: grog tempered.
A moderately hard fabric with an irregular fracture. It has been tempered with moderate amounts of medium-sized to very coarse angular grog fragments. A single body sherd in fabric group 6 survives from vessel 11.

Context	Fabric 1	Fabric 2	Fabric 3	Fabric 4	Fabric 5	Total
Trench 1						
[002]	1 (7)	-	1 (27)	-	-	2 (34)
[010], F.25	4 (3)	-	-	-	-	4 (3)
[011], F.23	9+ (23)	-	-	6+ (23)	1 (9)	16+ (55)
[018]	1 (2)	-	-	-	-	1 (2)
[027], F.3	12 (64)	-	-	-	-	12 (64)
[033]	2 (3)	-	-	-	-	2 (3)
[037], F.23	7 (19)	-	-	-	-	7 (19)
[038], F.24	-	-	2 (29)	-	-	2 (29)
[042], F.23	3 (16)	-	-	-	-	3 (16)
Trench 2						
[030], F.1	1 (2)	1 (5)	-	-	-	2 (7)
[061], F.16	32 (60)	-	-	-	-	32 (60)
Total	72+ (199)	1 (5)	3 (56)	6+ (23)	1 (9)	83+ (292)

TABLE 3. PREHISTORIC POTTERY ACCORDING TO FABRIC AND CONTEXT. WEIGHTS (IN GRAMS) GIVEN IN PARENTHESES

	Fabric 1	**Fabric 2**	**Fabric 3**	**Fabric 4**	**Fabric 5**	*Total*
Phase 1						
[010], F.25	4 (3)	-	-	-	-	
[011], F.23	9+ (23)	-	-	6+ (23)	1 (9)	
[037], F.23	7 (19)	-	-	-	-	
[038], F.24	-	-	2 (29)	-	-	
[042], F.23	3 (16)	-	-	-	-	
Sub-total	*23+ (61)*	*-*	*2 (29)*	*6+ (23)*	*1 (9)*	*32+ (122)*
Phase 2						
[027], F.3	12 (64)	-	-	-	-	
[033]	2 (3)	-	-	-	-	
Sub-total	*14 (67)*	*-*	*-*	*-*	*-*	*14 (67)*
Phase 3						
[018]	1 (2)	-	-	-	-	
Sub-total	*1 (2)*	*-*	*-*	*-*	*-*	*1 (2)*
Phase 4						
[002]	1 (7)	-	1 (27)	-	-	
Sub-total	*1 (7)*	*-*	*1 (27)*	*-*	*-*	*2 (34)*
Total	39+ (137)	-	3 (56)	6+ (23)	1 (9)	49+ (225)

TABLE 4. PREHISTORIC POTTERY FROM TRENCH 1 ACCORDING TO FABRIC AND PHASE.
WEIGHTS (IN GRAMS) GIVEN IN PARENTHESES

Discussion

Though small, the assemblage is regionally important, not least because so little later prehistoric pottery has been recovered from stratified contexts in the Usk valley region. All the pottery is of middle and late Iron Age date. When divided according to phase, it is evident that pottery had a more common currency on the site earlier in its history (middle Iron Age phases 1 and 2) than later. This pattern most probably relates to changes in the intensity of occupation, in this part of the site at least.

With one exception, a single sherd in fabric 1, all the pottery is in dark grey or black reduced fabrics. Vesicular mudstone fabrics (groups 1 and 4) are dominant throughout the sequence, these vessels being attributable to a clay source close to the Malvern Hills (Malvernian Group D: Morris 1982). The bulk of the pottery reaching Lodge Hill during the Iron Age was therefore of non-local manufacture, and may have come into the region along the same trade/exchange routes as Droitwich salt containers (see below). The presence of so much Malvernian-type pottery at Lodge Hill is something of a surprise, since the site lies at the limit of the distribution of this particular ceramic (Peacock 1968, Morris 1983). It is otherwise poorly represented in the Severn estuary region: only one sherd of Malvernian pottery was present in the extensive Iron Age assemblage from Thornwell Farm, near Chepstow (Woodward 1996, 44), for example. However, the distribution of this material may be more specific to the Usk valley than to the wider region, since vessels are otherwise known from Twyn-y-Gaer (Probert 1976), Abergavenny, Caerleon (Webster, in Manning 1993, 232) and perhaps Abernant (Anne Leaver pers. comm.). Only two sherds, in fabrics 2 (quartz and sandstone) and 5 (grog), could be local products. Sherds in similar quartz and sandstone fabrics to fabric 2 were common among later prehistoric vessels at Thornwell Farm (Woodward 1996), and in the report on this material it was suggested that the sandstone derived from local Triassic deposits (Welch & Trotter 1961). It is interesting to note the absence of Severn-valley calcite-tempered wares, which were produced at a variety of locations within the general Bristol Channel – Severn Estuary region (Allen 1998).

Few vessel profiles can be reconstructed, but it appears that the assemblage is composed of slack-shouldered jars of neutral or slightly closed form with simple, proto-beaded and beaded rims. All of the vessels are undecorated, though sherds from vessels 12, 14 and 15 show signs of burnish on their external surfaces. The absence of decorated vessels of Cunliffe's Lydney-Llanmelin style (2005, 630; Spencer's (1983) Class B), generally placed in the middle to late Iron Age, is notable, as is that of Malvern stamped ware. Both styles were recovered from the hillfort of Twyn-y-Gaer, near Abergavenny (Probert 1976, 115), though in very small quantities, and Lydney-Llanmelin wares from Llanmelin and Thornwell Farm to the east (Nash-Williams 1933, Woodward 1996, Spencer 1983). The range of vessel forms can be matched amongst the sizeable ceramic assemblage recovered during the excavations at Thornwell Farm (Woodward 1996).

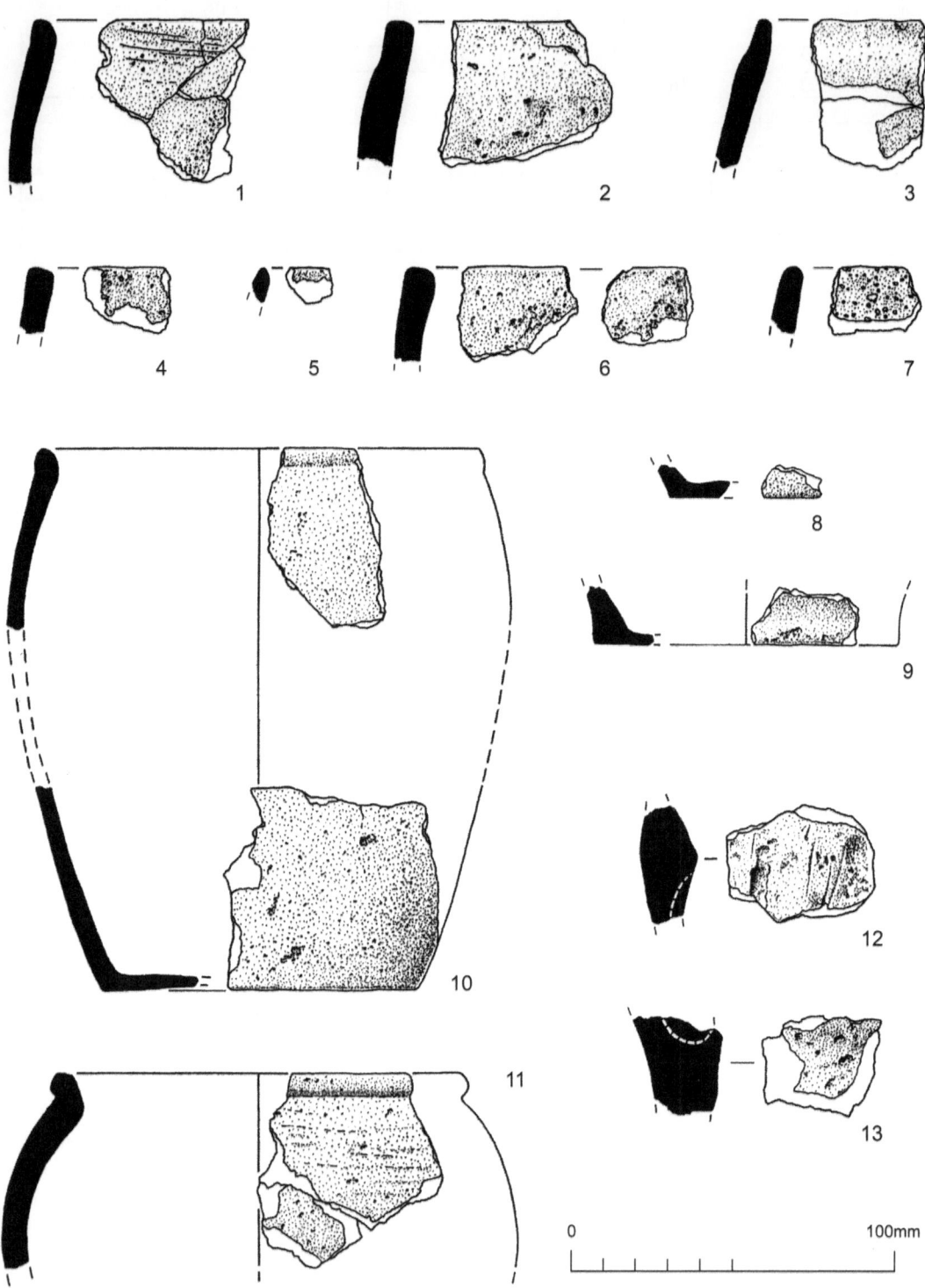

FIGURE 29. IRON AGE POTTERY (1-11) AND BRIQUETAGE (12-13). SEE TEXT FOR DESCRIPTION

Although only a small number of rim sherds (12 in total) are present within the Lodge Hill assemblage, it is possible to identify a sequence of development in rim form over time – from simple to proto-beaded and beaded. Vessels from phase 1 in Trench 1 have simple rims, as incidentally does that from the top of the primary fill in ditch F.16. These are seen in early/middle Iron Age contexts at Thornwell Farm (e.g. Group I: Woodward 1996, 39, fig. 26.21-2). Rims from phase 2 in Trench 1 are proto-beaded (e.g. vessel 15 from F.3, [027]). Identical proto-bead rims are seen as middle to late Iron Age at Thornwell Farm (e.g. Group K: Woodward 1996, 40-1, fig. 27.33-7), and are associated in one instance with a La Tène I brooch at Lodge Hill. From phase 4 is an ovoid jar with a well-developed beaded rim. Allen (1998, 37) suggests a 1st century AD date for calcite-tempered vessels of this form.

Both the proto-beaded and beaded rim jar forms at Lodge Hill are similar to Spencer's Class A limestone-tempered vessels, for which a 1st century AD date was originally proposed (Spencer 1983). Similar vessels were found at the hillforts of Sudbrook and Llanmelin (Nash-Williams 1933, 1939; Spencer 1983, fig. 1, 1-13), and in the fill of a palaeochannel on the Gwent foreshore at Magor Pill, here dated to the 1st century BC (Webster in Whittle 1989). In the light of evidence from Lodge Hill and Thornwell Farm, the late dating often given for proto-beaded rim jars is clearly in need of revision, and could be extended back to the middle Iron Age. Overall, such changes in rim morphology are minor and we are faced with a highly conservative potting tradition almost exclusively focussed on the production of simple ovoid jars.

There are few stratified/phased, well-excavated and fully reported Iron Age pottery assemblages within the region that might be compared with that from Lodge Hill. The best probably remains the assemblage from the farmstead site at Thornwell Farm, Chepstow (Woodward 1996). However, there may be problems with the dating of some of the ceramics from this site. In particular, the claimed late Bronze Age date for pottery from the pre-bank phase at Thornwell Farm is almost certainly erroneous: the key group (CG2) being better accommodated within the end of the early Iron Age and middle Iron Age (7th/6th – 5th/4th centuries BC). The illustrated examples of 'late Bronze Age' form types (types E-H; Woodward 1996, fig. 26) include simple ovoid, convex-profile jars that must be Iron Age, and probably not particularly early at that (with, perhaps, the exception of the type G cabled rim vessels (ibid., fig. 26, nos. 17-20) and a possible long-neck rim jar (ibid., fig. 26, no. 21) that might be placed in the early Iron Age proper). Similar problems occur with the 'early Iron Age' type D vessels. These are again simple ovoid, convex-profile jars that do not display any characteristics which might be regarded as specifically early Iron Age (ibid., fig. 25, nos. 9-12). The bulk of the later prehistoric pottery from Thornwell Farm, like that from Lodge Hill, probably dates to the 5th century BC onwards.

The Lodge Hill assemblage says very little about the economic status of the site, or of the range of productive activities taking place here. In terms of vessel function, direct evidence for the use of jars in open-fire cooking comes from traces of sooting present on vessels 13, 14 and 15, from phase 1 and 2 contexts in Trench 1. The vessels display a restricted range of sizes as well as forms: where reconstructable (e.g. vessels 4, 5 and 15) diameters fall within the 'small vessel' range of 150-200mm. That so few sherds are present from what was a relatively lengthy sequence of occupation suggests that pottery had a very restricted currency on the site, no doubt being complemented by a range of vessels manufactured from other materials (see, for example, the wooden tubs and bowls from the Breiddin: Britnell & Earwood in Musson 1991, 161-71).

Illustrated sherds (Fig. 29)
1. Rim. Vessel 8? Fabric Group 1. Trench 1, [037]
2. Rim. Vessel 13. Fabric Group 3. Trench 1, [038]
3. Rim. Vessel 14. Fabric Group 1. Trench 1, [042]
4. Rim. Vessel 8. Fabric Group 1. Trench 1, [011]
5. Rim. Vessel 7. Fabric Group 1. Trench 1, [010]
6. Rim. Vessel 1. Fabric Group 1. Trench 2, [061]
7. Rim. Vessel 2. Fabric Group 2. Trench 2, [030]
8. Base angle. Vessel 16. Fabric Group 1. Trench 1, [018]
9. Base angle. Vessel 4. Fabric Group 1. Trench 1, [002]
10. Rim, body and base. Vessel 15. Fabric Group 1. Trench 1, F.3, [027]
11. Rim and body. Vessel 5. Fabric Group 3. Trench 1, [002]

3.4. Droitwich briquetage
Joshua Pollard & Elaine Morris

Twenty-six fragments (161g) of Droitwich briquetage were recovered, all but two from Trench 1 (Fig. 29.12-13; Table 5). Sherds in both Droitwich briquetage fabric types 1 (sandy, marly) and 2 (similar clay matrix, but with varied amounts of organic temper) are present in roughly equal quantities (see Morris 1985 for detailed fabric description). The sherds are small and highly fragmented, many showing breakage along coil joins. No rim or base sherds are present, or at least identifiable, though in their original form these vessels are usually narrow and conical with flat-bases. The source for all these vessels is in the vicinity of the Droitwich brine springs, Worcestershire; the clay used in their manufacture coming from near-by deposits of Keuper Marl (ibid., 338-45). While there is an increase by weight and sherd number of fabric 1 during later phases of occupation within the interior – in fact, the reverse of what might be expected (ibid., 346-52) – the sample size is small and the pattern perhaps not meaningful.

Context	Fabric 1	Fabric 2	Total
Phase 1			
Trench 1, [011]	1 (10g)	2 (10g)	*3 (20g)*
Trench 1, [042]	-	3 (32g)	*3 (32g)*
Trench 1, [048]	-	4 (3g)	*4 (3g)*
Phase 2			
Trench 1, F.3, [027]	1 (14g)	1 (4g)	*2 (18g)*
Phase 4			
Trench 1, [002]	11 (36g)	1 (26g)	*12 (62g)*
Trench 2, F.1, [080]	2 (26g)	-	*2 (26g)*
Total	*15 (86g)*	*11 (75g)*	*26 (161g)*

TABLE 5. DROITWICH BRIQUETAGE BY CONTEXT, PHASE AND FABRIC

Production of salt containers at Droitwich began around the 6th century BC and continued up to the Roman conquest; the scale of production and the extent of distribution increasing from the 5th century BC onwards (Morris 1985). The Lodge Hill material spans a wide date range. The earliest pieces come from secure phase 1 contexts in the interior, pre-dating the deposition of the La Tène I brooch; while the the latest (including large pieces with fresh break surfaces) are associated with late Iron Age and Roman ceramics from phase 4.

Droitwich briquetage has been recovered from both hillfort and non-hillfort sites in the Severn-Avon region, including Twyn-y-Gaer (Probert 1976) and Sudbrook (Nash-Williams 1939; Morris 1985, 350). Its southerly distribution is closely tied to that of middle and late Iron Age Malvernian pottery. The presence of Droitwich briquetage in Iron Age contexts at Lodge Hill is somewhat unexpected since it lies c.15-20km beyond the currently recognised distribution of this material (Morris 1985, fig. 6; 2001, fig. 122). Its presence is all the more marked because of the apparent absence of briquetage from other excavated hillforts in the region, at Llanmelin (Nash-Williams 1933) and Coed y Bwnydd (Babbidge 1977), and from the enclosed settlement at Thornwell Farm (Woodward 1996, 45). While this may be a reflection of the relative 'status' of individual sites, it could equally indicate participation in differing networks of exchange.

3.5. Roman pottery
Ray Howell & Joshua Pollard

The following report has been produced on the basis of identifications kindly provided by Dr Peter Webster. 17 sherds of Roman pottery were recovered during the excavations, all but three from the upper levels in Trench 1 [002] (Fig. 30). Much of the material is small and quite heavily abraded, making detailed comment and analysis impossible. Nonetheless, given the context of the material, it remains of value in assisting understanding of post-Iron Age activity on the site.

There are three sherds of samian, including one small fragment from [002] of South Gaulish manufacture and probably of 1st century date, and a highly abraded sherd from a decorated bowl (from Tr. 2, [060]) perhaps of the 2nd century. Amongst the coursewares, there is a rim from a Black Burnished flanged bowl of a form that belongs to AD270 or later (probably 4th century), and two joining sherds of mortarium from the Cirencester area that are likely to be of 3rd or 4th century date.

Whilst the identified sherds cover the span of the Roman occupation within the region, there is a slight bias towards the 3rd and 4th centuries, particularly amongst the material from the interior of the site.

3.6. Medieval pottery
Rick Peterson & Joshua Pollard

A single flat-topped rim in a medieval fabric came from [033] in Trench 1, the sherd being intrusive within this context. The fabric, with plentiful medium-sized particles of well-rounded quartzite and some red iron ore, suggests local manufacture and a probable 12th or 13th century date.

3.7. Brick and tile
Joshua Pollard

25 pieces of Roman tile and brick were recovered. All the pieces were small (<80mm in maximum dimension) and most quite heavily abraded. Of 10 fragments from [002] in Trench 1, four appear to be pieces of *imbrex*, ranging in thickness between 9-15mm. One is flanged and another has an irregular (post-firing?) groove on the inner surface. Another piece, with a thickness of 25mm is perhaps a fragment of *tegula*. From the upper rubble fill of ditch F.16 [059] came 14 fragments from a single *imbrex* in a soft fabric. A small piece of brick in a dense dull reddish-brown fabric from [012] in Trench 3 may be either Roman or modern.

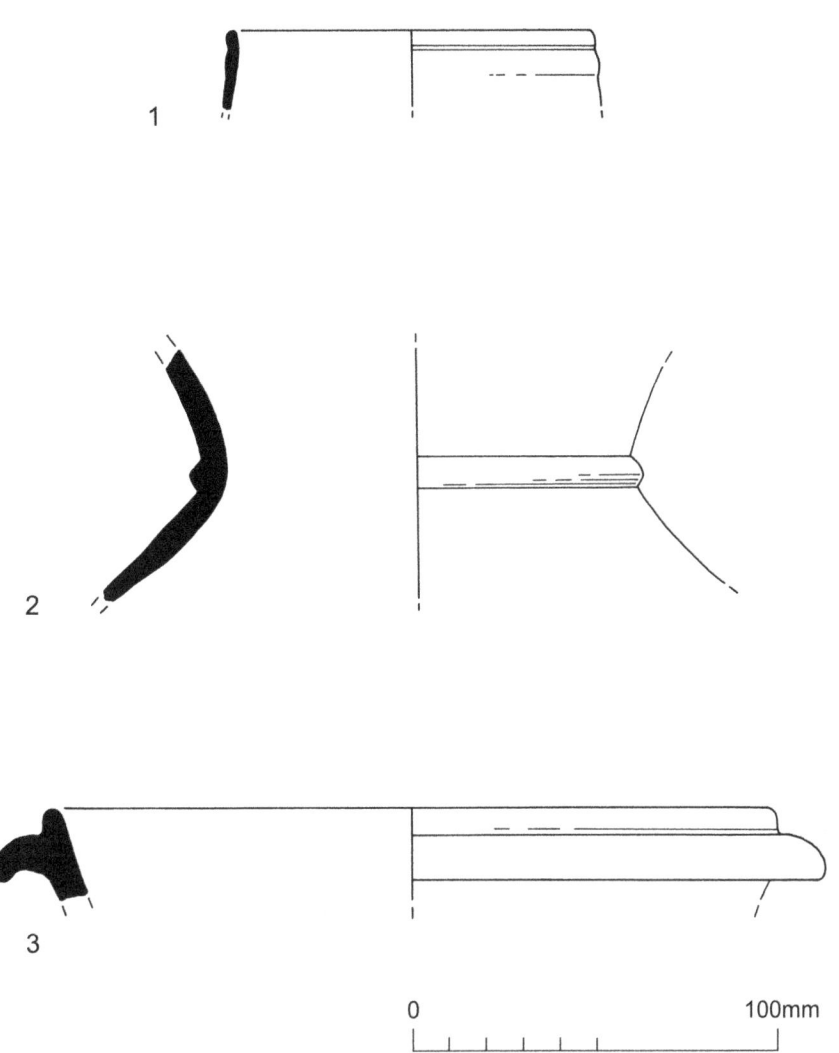

FIGURE 30. ROMAN POTTERY

The brick and tile ranges in colour from pale orange to reddish-orange and a dull reddish-brown; and is in a range of sand- and grog- tempered fabrics (details held in archive).

Given the small number of pieces recovered, it is unlikely that these indicate the presence of a substantial building on the site. Those pieces from the interior could even have been introduced along with manure, if limited cultivation is inferred. Whatever the mechanism of their introduction, they do provide additional evidence for Roman-period activity within the hillfort.

3.8. Fired clay
Joshua Pollard

A small quantity of fired clay came from contexts in Trenches 1 (70+ pieces, weighing 113g) and 3 (four pieces, weighing 8g) (Table 6). Almost half of this material by weight was recovered from context [002], and is perhaps associated with Roman phase activity. The material is in four distinct fabrics, the most common (1) comprising unsorted local clay without any visible additions. Many of these pieces probably derive from hearth bases and the 'accidental' firing of artificial or natural clay surfaces. Fabrics 2 and 3 are represented in each instance by single pieces. The fabrics are as follows:

1. Unsorted local clay. Pinkish grey to reddish-brown. Fine sand and very rare voids.

2. Moderately hard. Moderate quantities of sand and fine clay pellets. Reddish-orange.

3. Moderately hard. Abundant small laminar voids (from poor mixing of clay) and common rounded and sub-angular sandstone pieces. Reddish-orange to buff. River clay?

Context	Fabric 1	Fabric 2	Fabric 3	Total
Trench 1, [002]	24+ (48g)	1 (2g)	1 (8g)	26+ (58g)
Trench 1, [008]	1 (2g)	-	-	1 (2g)
Trench 1, [011]	7 (25g)	-	-	7 (25g)
Trench 1, [017]	1 (1g)	-	-	1 (1g)
Trench 1, [018]	17+ (11g)	-	-	17+ (11g)
Trench 1, [027]	1 (3g)	-	-	1 (3g)
Trench 1, [028]	2 (2g)	-	-	2 (2g)
Trench 1, [033]	3 (3g)	-	-	3 (3g)
Trench 1, [037]	3+ (4g)	-	-	3+ (4g)
Trench 1, [042]/[048]	2 (4g)	-	-	2 (4g)
Trench 3, [055]	4 (8g)	-	-	4 (8g)
Total	65+ (111g)	1 (2g)	1 (8g)	74+ (121g)

TABLE 6. FIRED CLAY ACCORDING TO CONTEXT AND FABRIC

All the pieces are small and highly fragmented. While some of the larger examples with partially reduced cores and inner surfaces could be part of oven or furnace superstructures, the bulk of this material is clearly non-structural. No definite fragments of daub were recovered.

3.9. Worked flint
Joshua Pollard

Only two pieces of worked flint were recovered, both from Trench 1. These comprise the distal end of a blade or flake with marginal retouch from [017] and a burnt fragment of core from [002]. Heavily patinated, the retouched blade/flake is perhaps of Mesolithic or Neolithic date. They do not constitute convincing evidence for sustained earlier prehistoric activity on the hill, and might anyway have been brought onto the site along with stone or other introduced materials during the period of Iron Age occupation.

3.10. Other worked stone
Joshua Pollard

In addition to the flint, nine pieces of worked stone were recovered from Iron Age and later contexts. All but one of these (a pebble rubber from Trench 2) came from deposits in Trench 1. The pieces comprise two flaked sandstone discs, three hammerstones/pounders, two rubbers and two grooved blocks (Fig. 31).

Both of the sandstone discs were recovered from [010]. The smaller of these is made on a tabular piece of micaceous sandstone which was flaked into shape and the edges then ground smooth, the grinding only partially obliterating the flake scars (Fig. 31.5). The larger example is roughly flaked and perhaps unfinished (Fig. 31.4). Flaked discs of this kind are known from Neolithic (e.g. Piggott 1962, 48-9), Iron Age (e.g. Laws in Sharples 1991a, 232-3) and Medieval contexts; and locally large numbers have been recovered from the multi-period site at Abernant 4.5km east of Lodge Hill, on the opposite side of the Usk valley (Anne Leaver pers. comm.). Larger examples may have served as pot lids, but with diameters under 65mm those from Lodge Hill are likely to have had a different function, perhaps as small stands or weights.

The three hammerstones/pounders are all on unmodified sandstone pebbles collected from river gravel deposits. In each instance evidence of use is limited to signs of battering on one or both ends of the pebble. Two examples, from [001] and [011], are broken, the third, from [002], complete (Fig. 31.2). These may have been employed in a variety of tasks, from shaping and dressing quern stones, rubbers or other stone artefacts (such as the flaked sandstone discs) to preparing plant fibres and processing ore.

A small rubber from [060] in Trench 2 is also on an unmodified sandstone pebble. Two sides are flattened and smoothed through use. A fragment of a second rubber in a coarse-grained sandstone from [011] has one flat surface ground smooth, and another slightly concave with traces of pecking.

Of uncertain function are two grooved slabs from [002]. The first is a sub-rectangular sandstone slab with a single grooved line running diagonally across one surface (Fig. 31.1); the second a block with a deep U-shaped curvilinear groove on one face and traces of shallow linear grooves on the other (Fig. 31.3).

In addition to the obviously worked pieces, fragments of quartz conglomerate were recovered from [011]. Deriving from the local Upper Old Red Sandstone, this rock is known to have been used during the Roman period for the production of rotary querns (e.g. at Whitton: Welfare in Jarrett & Wrathmell 1981, 222).

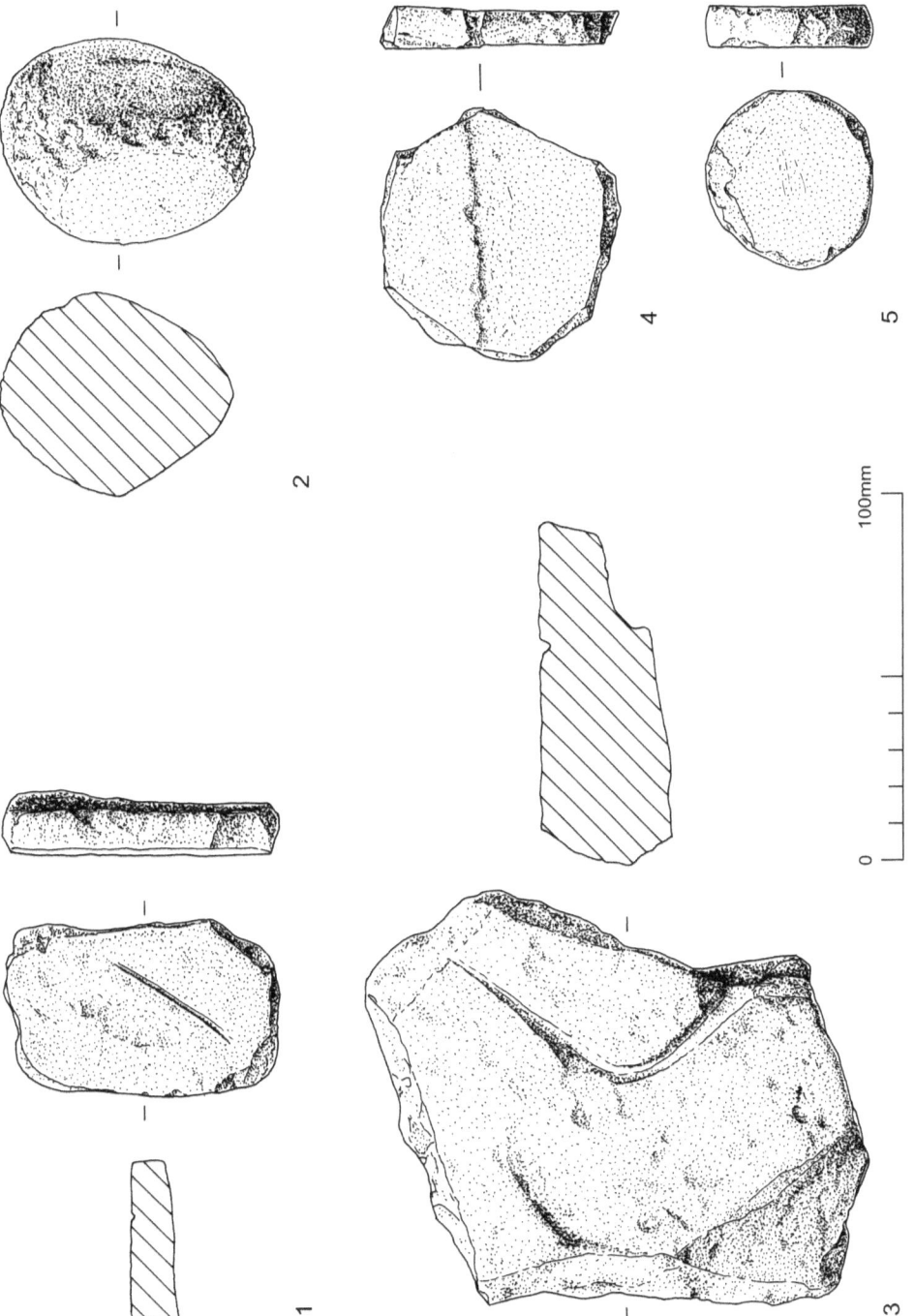

Figure 31. Worked stone: 1, 3. grooved slabs (Trench 1, [002]); 2. hammerstone/pounder (Trench 1, [002]); 4-5. flaked discs (Trench 1, [010])

4. Environmental Evidence
Ruth Young

Trench	Context	No. of Fragments	Weight (g.)	Comments
1	[002]	5	2.7	Long bone; 2 skull?
1	[011]	multiple	46.0	Long bones; 3-4 skull?; 1 rib; 1 pelvis?; unfused tibia articulation (sheep); astragalus (sheep)
1	[017]	multiple	62.6	Long bones; 3 phalanges (sheep); 1 pelvis (sheep)
1	[018]	multiple	14.4	Long bones; 1 pelvis?
1	[026]	3	1.2	
1	[027]	8	1.0	
1	[033]	1	0.3	
1	[037]	multiple	36.3	4 carpal/tarsal; long bone; 1 phalange (chicken)
1	[042]	3	2.7	
1	[042]/[048]	2	0.2	
1	[048]	multiple	4.8	
2	[061]	7	1.4	1 skull?
2	[080]	11	2.7	
2	[082]	5	0.2	
Total			176.5	

TABLE 7. CALCINED ANIMAL BONE: QUANTITIES AND IDENTIFICATION

4.1. Animal bone

Because of the acidic nature of the soils, only highly calcined bone survived. The majority of this came from phase 1 and 2 deposits within Trench 1 (Table 7).

The bone is very fragmented, the vast majority being broken pieces of 1cm^2 or smaller, with breakage appearing to have taken place before deposition. No teeth or teeth fragments were noted, and all pieces, whether identifiable to species, element or simply type of bone, are compatible with animals the size of sheep or smaller. While there are fragments from skull and pelvis, the majority of bone material is from long bones, and almost all the identified material is from the robust lower limbs such as phalanges or astragali. The only species identified were sheep and chicken, and clearly at least one young sheep is represented here.

4.2. Charred plant remains and charcoal

Given the major research questions leading the excavations, namely the function of the hillfort and the potential for contact between the hillfort and the neighbouring sites, the recovery and analysis of archaeobotanical material was seen as an essential component of the project. Macrobotanical plant remains, whether wood charcoal or grains and seeds, have the potential to address such questions in this context. For example, recovering large amounts of charred cereals from potential grain stores could give insight into the nature of agricultural storage. Further, weed seeds associated with crops, or the presence of wild plants can shed light on seasonal occupation, and the presence of exotic items may suggest trade connections. Wood charcoal can be of great importance in learning about local tree cover during occupation of a site; imported wood can again suggest trade networks; and wood is a major fuel for activities such as metal-working, and as such can shed light on techniques, fuel preferences and deforestation over time. As Jones (1996, 29) notes, the importance of plant management, be it crop or tree was vital for the Iron Age economy. It was intended that all these issues should be addressed through the analysis and identification of a suitable macrobotanical assemblage.

Methods
Routine sampling for environmental material was carried out during the excavations. On-site sampling comprised collection of up to 30 litres of soil from selected features or layers. Charcoal was also recovered manually during the course of the excavation.

Bulk samples were processed using an Ankara style flotation machine, with a minimum 300 micron sieve, and sorted by hand. Wood charcoal preparation and identification followed standard procedure, namely examining a range of pieces 2mm^3 and larger, splitting them according to transverse, radial longitudinal and

Trench	Context	Wood charcoal present	Identifiable	Other material noted
1	[002]	no		Pink clay soil
1	[010]	yes	yes	
1	[011]	yes	yes	Cremated bone
1	[017]	yes	yes	
1	[018]	yes	yes	
1	[026]	yes	yes	
1	[027]	yes	yes	
1	[028]	yes	yes	
1	[033]	yes	yes	
1	[035]	yes	yes	
1	[037]	yes	yes	
1	[042]	yes	yes	Bone fragments
1	[045]	yes	yes	
1	[048]	yes	yes	1 grain wheat
2	[061]	yes	no (smears only)	
2	[076]	yes	no (smears only)	
2	[080]	yes	yes	
2	[084]	yes	yes	
2	[086]	yes	no (too small)	
3	[043]	yes	yes	
3	[055]	yes	yes	
3	[057]	yes	no (too small)	
3	[064]	yes	yes	
3	[083]	yes	no (too small)	

TABLE 8. SUMMARY OF PRESENCE WOOD CHARCOAL IN ALL SAMPLES PROCESSED

tangential longitudinal sections, and examining them under magnification up to x100 (Dimbleby 1978; Thompson 1994, 20). Identification of wood charcoal was carried out using the keys of Ilic (1991) and Schweingruber (1978) alongside reference material.

Table 8 lists all the samples recovered by context, with the presence of all the wood charcoal, showing whether it could be considered for identification.

Results and Discussion
Cereals and weeds
Table 8 shows that only one identifiable seed or grain was recovered from the processed samples at Lodge Hill Camp. This absence is interesting for a number of reasons, and certainly should not be taken as an indication of an absence of cereals either around or on the site itself.

The single identifiable grain of wheat (*Triticum* sp.) was recovered from Trench 1, context [048]. As this grain was distorted, and had a partial covering of a gritty concretion, identification was to genus only. Trench 1 was positioned inside the main earthwork system of the hillfort, and noted by the excavators to be in an area of considerable bioturbation, particularly from root action.

Context [048] is a discrete layer of purple-brown clay loam, lying over the base of the quarry. This layer has been interpreted by the excavators as possibly an occupation soil, and in addition to the grain, contained stones, wood charcoal and baked clay or daub pieces. The presence of wood charcoal, although in fragments too small to be identified, might be indicative of domestic burning in some way associated with cereals.

However, it is also necessary to consider at least some of the reasons why no more grain has been recovered and identified. One of the most obvious reasons is likely to be the nature and function of the areas and contexts excavated. In Trench 1, context [033] is a floor within a structure, suggested by the excavators to belong to an ancillary building, possibly a granary or shed. Given the complete absence of grain from this surface, and relatively small amount of wood charcoal, it is unlikely to be a granary.

Other buildings in Trench 1, indicated by the numerous post-holes were clearly not being used for any grain storage function, nor were they or any associated hearth areas being used for domestic food processing and preparation. While the terraces assigned to Phase 3 (Trench 1, contexts [008], [017] and [018]) are thought to have had an agricultural purpose within the enclosure itself, the absence of any grain from these contexts suggests that they were not cleared by burning.

The disturbed nature of the soils within Trench 1 may also be a contributing factor to the absence of charred seeds and grain. While charred material is generally resistant to biological action within the soil, it is susceptible to mechanical breakdown. The presence of dense modern vegetation in this area, with the accompanying root systems necessarily results in material being lost. Smaller, more fragile plant remains, such as cereal grain and chaff, are likely to be broken down more readily than larger and more robust types of wood charcoal.

As Trench 2 was placed to cut across the inner ditch and bank of the hillfort, the absence of grain is not altogether surprising. However, ditches are often used as dumping areas for domestic waste, and burnt bone was recovered from [082] within the bank structure. All we can conclude from this is that if domestic cooking waste was being dumped in this ditch, Trench 2 missed any deposits of plant food rubbish.

Trench 3, positioned over part of the western entrance to the hilllfort is again unlikely to have incorporated any occupation areas within its boundaries. Although the dumping of household waste around the entrance may have been a possibility, the recovery of cereals from such an area is unlikely, and again, the absence of grain, chaff and so forth should not be surprising.

Therefore, it is likely that the presence of dense vegetation on the site over a lengthy period of time has resulted in the breakdown of fragile plant remains, and the nature of the features and areas excavated are both contributing factors to this absence of plant macroremains other than wood charcoal.

Wood charcoal
In contrast to the almost total absence of weeds and cereals, wood charcoal has been recovered in some quantity from a range of contexts across the site. Table 9 lists the identifications of wood charcoal from all three trenches. Woodland management is well known from a number of sites throughout Britain, and in particular from work around the Somerset Levels (Rackham 1977), where hazel is known to have been managed through a form of coppicing. Pollen analysis from Cefn Graeanog shows a very clear and long lasting episode of woodland clearance during the 1st millennium BC (Bell 1996, 8). Woodland clearance during the Iron Age is associated with increasing agriculture and the demand for fuel for metalworking. Timber is also crucial for construction, and hillforts in Wales (and elsewhere) are known to have made use of timber as support structures in the construction of the ramparts (Savory 1976, 245). Lodge Hill Camp is no exception to this, as the excavations in Trench 2, the inner ditch and bank, make clear. For all these reasons the recovery, identification and analysis of wood charcoal assemblages is very important.

Range of species and distribution of wood charcoal
A total of 473 pieces of wood charcoal were considered identifiable, and of these, 449 were assigned to genus or species (Table 9). Oak (61% of identified fragments) clearly dominates the assemblage, followed by hazel (19% of identified fragments). This is not really surprising in an assemblage from a British site of this period (e.g. Boyd 1988), and suggests exploitation of local woodland for fuel and construction purposes. The other woody types are present in relatively small numbers, and show a range of trees and shrubs. In terms of quantity, the other types identified in significant quantity are cherry and gorse (both 5% of identified material).

The number of identifiable wood charcoal fragments recovered was clearly greatest from [011] in Trench 1 (the fill of the quarry F.23), with smaller concentrations recovered from [037] and [042], both in Trench 1, also quarry fill from the western section. The other context with a significant concentration of wood charcoal is [055], Trench 3, which is interpreted as a layer of material used to increase the bank height. There is no clear reason why these contexts should have a greater number of larger (and therefore more identifiable) pieces of wood charcoal, although the soil used to fill the quarry may have come from the same area, and may have previously been associated with burning, perhaps even land clearance (Jones 1996).

'Cremation' wood
Within [011] in Trench 1 (the fill of quarry, F.23) a marked concentration of calcined animal bone, possibly a cremation, was recovered, along with associated wood charcoal. This wood charcoal was identified as gorse (23 fragments identified), thus accounting for its significance in the assemblage. Given the abundance and range of wood charcoal from trees across the site, it must be assumed that gorse was selected specifically for this 'cremation', and this raises some interesting questions about fuel use for such a dedicated purpose. Again, gorse is likely to have been readily available, but its almost total absence from the rest of the assemblage suggests that it was not a type selected by choice for any other purpose.

Iron-working slag and wood
A number of iron artefacts were recovered from Trench 1, along with a quantity of metalworking debris. The presence of this waste suggests that iron-working was taking place on site, although no actual furnaces were located. 14 fragments of charcoal from [010] and [028] – both contexts that produced iron-working debris – were identifiable, with hazel being the dominant species. This

Trench 1 Context	010	011	017	018	026	027	028	033	035	037	042	045	048	Total
Species														
Alder	-	-	1	-	1	-	-	1	-	-	1	-	-	*4*
Birch	-	2	-	-	-	-	1	-	-	-	-	-	-	*3*
Hazel	2	48	2	2	-	-	4	1	-	9	7	1	-	*76*
Hawthorn	-	3	1	-	-	-	-	-	-	-	1	-	-	*5*
Ash	-	-	-	-	1	-	1	-	-	-	-	-	-	*2*
Ivy	-	4	-	-	1	-	-	-	-	1	-	-	-	*6*
Holly	-	6	-	-	-	-	-	-	-	1	-	-	-	*7*
Pine	-	-	-	-	-	?1	-	-	-	-	-	-	-	*?1*
Cherry	-	17	-	-	-	-	-	3	-	-	3	-	-	*23*
Oak	-	133	2	3	1	2	-	17	2	24	39	2	1	*226*
Willow	-	7	-	-	-	-	2	-	-	-	-	-	-	*9*
Rowan	-	-	-	-	-	-	1	-	-	1	-	-	-	*2*
Gorse	-	23	-	-	-	-	1	-	-	-	-	-	-	*24*
Unidentified	-	11	-	1	-	-	2	3	-	1	2	-	-	*20*
Total	*2*	*254*	*6*	*6*	*4*	*3*	*12*	*25*	*2*	*37*	*53*	*3*	*1*	*408*

Trench 2 Context	080	084												
Species														
Alder	-	-												-
Birch	-	-												-
Hazel	2	-												*2*
Hawthorn	-	-												-
Ash	-	-												-
Ivy	-	-												-
Holly	-	-												-
Pine	-	-												-
Cherry	-	-												-
Oak	7	1												*8*
Willow	-	-												-
Rowan	-	-												-
Gorse	-	-												-
Unidentified	1	-												*1*
Total	*10*	*1*												*11*

Trench 3 Context	043	055	064											
Species														
Alder	-	-	-											-
Birch	-	2	-											*2*
Hazel	1	8	-											*9*
Hawthorn	-	-	-											-
Ash	-	-	-											-
Ivy	-	-	-											-
Holly	-	-	-											-
Pine	-	-	-											-
Cherry	-	-	-											-
Oak	-	39	1											*40*
Willow	-	-	-											-
Rowan	-	-	-											-
Gorse	-	-	-											-
Unidentified	-	3	-											*3*
Total	*1*	*52*	*1*											*54*

TABLE 9. WOOD CHARCOAL IDENTIFICATIONS

is consistent with wood charcoal associated with iron working in Britain, where hazel and oak seem to be the preferred wood types.

Construction wood
Samples were taken from a number of construction contexts, and the wood identified from these provides an idea of the types used in construction. In Trench 1, [033] (a stone spread at the southerly entrance to a small enclosure), [017] (a stone and soil spread which may be part of a small enclosure or remnants of an up-cast bank), and [027] (the upper fill of ditch F.3), could all be considered as part of general construction events. While [033] has a clear concentration of oak, there is a mix of types from all these contexts.

Trench 2 is clearly of interest for the light it sheds on the construction of the enclosures. Timber is known to have been used for rampart frameworks, and the wood recovered from [080] and [084] was identified where possible. Oak was again the dominant wood, providing a readily available, strong timber. Oak also dominated the material recovered from contexts related to construction in Trench 3. In both [055] and [064] oak was significant.

Conclusions
The archaeobotanical assemblage from Lodge Hill is almost entirely made up of wood charcoal. A single wheat grain was recovered and identified, and no other weed seeds, grains or chaff were noted. This may be due to the type of areas excavated, or may be a product of mechanical disturbance across the site at work on fragile remains.

Of the wood charcoal recovered and identified, oak and hazel dominated the assemblage, which is typical of a British Iron Age site. Of interest is the presence of gorse in association with a possible cremation, and a very small number of oak fragments in the same context as iron-working debris, the former because it gives us some insight into fuel selection for cremations, and the latter because it confirms existing knowledge of fuel selection for charcoal making for iron-working. Oak also dominates the material recovered and identified from contexts associated with construction, particularly those of the inner bank and ditch.

List of Names

Botanical Name	English Name
Triticum sp.	wheat
Alnus glutinosa	alder
Betula sp.	birch
Corylus avellana	hazel
Crategus sp.	hawthorn
Fraxinus excelsio	ash
Hedera helix	ivy
Ilex aquifolium	holly
Pinus sp.	pine
Prunus avium/padus	wild cherry or bird cherry
Quercus sp.	oak
Salix sp.	willow
Sorbus aucuparia	rowan
Ulex sp.	gorse

5. Discussion: Lodge Hill Camp and the hillforts of Gwent

Joshua Pollard, Ray Howell, Adrian Chadwick & Lesley McFadyen

From the evidence of the earthworks alone, it was apparent before excavation that Lodge Hill was a complex monument embodying a lengthy history of construction and occupation. It was also evident that a full understanding of the hillfort could not be achieved through what was a very limited excavation focussed on just the western third of the site. But, while the 2000 excavations must be regarded as a compromised, if targeted, sample of the rich archaeological deposits that make up the site, the results should not be downplayed. In addition to providing important information relating to the character and intensity of activity within the hillfort during the Iron Age and after, the excavations have greatly enhanced our understanding of the constructional history of the monument. It is now possible to provide some detail on the changing character of human activity on Lodge Hill during the later prehistoric, Roman and, perhaps, immediate post-Roman periods.

5.1. Later prehistoric activity and the creation of the hillfort

Summary and discussion of the excavated sequence
If not introduced at a later date, the two worked flints from Trench 1 hint at visits to the hill during the Mesolithic or Neolithic. The distinctive saddleback would also have provided a suitable location for early Bronze Age round barrows/cairns, though none have been identified. Even if there is little evidence for pre-Iron Age activity, we can envisage the hill as a known, and named, landmark by the time that the hillfort was constructed.

It was towards the end of the early or beginning of the middle Iron Age that the topography of the hill was radically transformed through the digging of quarry pits and the creation of an encircling stone and timber-laced bank. The earliest features encountered within the interior are the quarry hollow F.23 and two adjacent rock-cut scoops, F.24 and 25. While the former provided stone that was used in the construction of the inner bank, the latter created level platforms for buildings set within the slope of the hillcrest. Occupation of sorts followed immediately on from this building activity, as indicated by finds of pottery, briquetage, worked stone (discs, a pounder and rubber), and metalworking debris from smithing within the fills of the quarry scoops. Pre-dating by some margin the deposition of a La Tène I brooch in a shallow ditch cut into these fills, this activity most likely dates to the 5th century BC. Whether such occupation was permanent or intermittent remains uncertain, but the quantities of material culture from the Iron Age deposits are by no means great.

At a later date a small ditched and banked enclosure (comprising ditches F.20, F.3 and bank spread [017]) was created within this part of the hillfort interior. This enclosure was entered via a narrow southerly entrance, paved with cobbles, around which deposits of cremated animal bone were placed. The ditch was redefined on at least one occasion and finally deliberately backfilled with rubble. Fresh sherds of pottery from a single vessel, fragments of briquetage and the iron La Tène I brooch (with pin fastened) were contained within the backfill. They could represent deliberate 'decommissioning' deposits. Early La Tène brooches were frequently employed as votives, and the context of the Lodge Hill example in a ditch terminal fits a broader pattern of preferential deposition of middle Iron Age brooches in boundary contexts (Haselgrove 1997, 56). The brooch itself probably dates to the first half of the 4th century BC.

Given the limited extent of the excavation, it is difficult to determine what this diminutive enclosure enclosed (the ditches are certainly too straight to be roundhouse gullies), though it perhaps defined an area in which iron-working or some other specialist activity took place. There were various post settings within and outside the enclosure, some possibly forming elements of four-post structures. One group at least, set within the lee of the inner hillfort bank, defined a small rectangular structure, 2.2 x 3.0+m. This was solidly built with an internal paved surface. The presence of this 'floor' implies the superstructure was not suspended in the manner of a raised granary, so some other function must be envisaged. It was too small to have acted as a house or shelter and anyway lacks associated occupation deposits. Other middle Iron Age rectangular structures are known within the region, for example at Goldcliff and the Gwent Euro Park site near Magor on the Gwent Levels, several kilometres to the east (Bell *et al.* 2000, Nayling, pers. comm.). However, these were larger, at c.8 x 6m, and used as part of seasonal exploitation of grazing land on the Levels. The rectangular shape of such buildings defined them as different from the 'cosmologically loaded' format of contemporary roundhouses (Oswald 1997, Parker Pearson 1996, Fitzpatrick 1994). Various ancillary functions can, and have been, suggested for square and rectangular structures in the British Iron Age, including their use for mortuary practices (Ellison & Drewett 1971; Bell *et al.* 2000, 72). In this respect, it is surely significant that no convincing case can be made for the presence of roundhouses in the western part of the hillfort. Indeed, much of the activity in this area may have been more 'industrial' or 'specialized', than 'domestic', in character.

A major transformation in the way this part of the interior, and perhaps the hillfort as a whole, was utilized comes during phase 3, dating to the end of the middle or beginning of the late Iron Age. Occupation appears to cease and a series of narrow terraces were laid out across this area. This is not abandonment as such, but a change in the utilization of the interior, most likely representing an episode of 'garden plot' cultivation. The only material culture associated with this is a single sherd of pottery (at less than 2g almost certainly residual) and some fragments of fired clay.

A scatter of pottery (including sherds from a late Iron Age bead-rim jar), briquetage and other material in soil deposits overlying the terraces implies renewed occupation on a limited scale during the late Iron Age. Activity continues, albeit perhaps intermittently, in the Roman period and is associated with a lightly-built timber structure. The significance of this 'late phase' activity will be considered further below.

While, as a consequence of the excavation strategy, the sequence revealed in the interior cannot be linked stratigraphically to that of the enclosing defences, it is highly likely that the digging of quarry F.23 was undertaken to acquire material for the creation of inner bank F.1. Associated with this must also be the first phase features in Trench 3.

The inner bank F.1 was comprised of earth and rubble dumps perhaps reinforced by timber lacing, the impression being of a cellular or compartmentalized structure. Given the volume of stone rubble in ditch F.16, it is likely that the ramparts of the inner bank would originally have stood at least a metre or so higher than at present. It was not possible in the limited timescale to investigate the bank in as sufficient detail as might be wished. Many of the stone and earth structures within it only became apparent in section once most of the bank had been taken down to the old ground surface/natural, and what appeared in plan to be a relatively undifferentiated mass of stone and earth proved to be a complicated series of 'walling', dumping and re-modelling episodes. Cutting relatively narrow sections through Iron Age ramparts has long been a favoured excavation technique. Although the limited timescale of the Lodge Hill excavations allowed no other means of excavating the bank, in retrospect it would have been more informative to open a linear trench along the rampart. Then, working in plan and with a 'single-context' recording methodology, it would perhaps be possible to excavate and record in reverse the complicated series of events and episodes that made up the biography of the bank. Such an experimental approach should certainly be adopted on any future hillfort excavations, either at Lodge Hill itself or on another site.

The revetment stones of F.15 may have had a functional purpose, in that they might have served to limit erosion on the steepest part of the slope. However, they may also have given the impression that most of the slope behind ditch F.16 was a human construct. In fact, the excavation showed that it was largely a natural slope, albeit possibly terraced in places, but the addition of stone may have suggested to outsiders that the ramparts were even taller and more massive than they were.

Since much of the stone and earth used in the construction of F.1 probably came from internal quarries, ditch F.16 is best regarded as a secondary feature associated with the initial stages of multivallation. The ditch cut was initially massive and V-shaped, making use of the natural slope and the geological interface between the marl and solid sandstone. Material dug from this was probably used to create the simple dump-construction earthen bank F.31. No dateable material came from the primary fills, but several sherds of middle/late Iron Age pottery were recovered from the lower fills of a broad, shallow re-cut. Earlier re-cutting episodes might be represented, but ditch re-cuts are notoriously difficult to spot, for if carried out on a regular basis they will effectively be archaeologically invisible, the ditches becoming slightly deeper and wider each time. With regard to Iron Age ditches, it is possible that visible re-cuts are the result of more episodic re-cutting, perhaps associated with major social events and/or reaffirmations of claims to the land (q.v. Chadwick 1999).

It was not possible to determine if the thick rubble deposits filling the re-cut ditch were the result of sudden collapse due to erosion, or deliberate slighting. The latter must remain a possibility. Iron Age pottery was recovered from deposits preceding the rubble collapse deposits, and Romano-British pottery and tile from one of the upper rubble deposits themselves. This suggests that the rubble collapse episodes were linked to a change in the nature of inhabitation on the site, and may even be indirect evidence for Roman slighting of the defences.

Sufficient of the western entrance (Trench 3) was investigated to show that in its original form it comprised a low stone-revetted bank incorporating a recessed area or 'guard chamber' at the rear. The bank may have supported a timber framework and gate structure. It was of cellular construction with a projecting hornwork at the front. While its cellular character perhaps resulted from successive enlargement and lengthening of the entrance passage, it could equally reflect a particular constructional style (note the evidence for compartmentalization seen in Trench 2). Overall, the arrangement bears a striking similarity to that of the period III-IV south-eastern entrance at Dinorben, Denbighshire (Gardner & Savory 1964, 20-24), creating a narrow passage-way with flanking 'chambers' set at the rear (Fig. 32). The entrance was both 'clean' and apparently short-lived. There was no sign of contemporary traffic wear, nor of any occupation: pottery and other material culture being absent. In fact, there is no evidence that the entrance was particularly used during the Iron Age. Furthermore, the whole entrance was apparently soon blocked when the inner bank was heightened through the addition of clay and stone dumps. This simple earthen rampart was perhaps faced by stonework, or supported a stone superstructure.

Why should the western entrance be so little used and so short-lived? It certainly provided an easy route of access into the hillfort along the gently sloping ridge to the south-west, and the evidence of occupation and other activity within Trench 1 shows that the western third of the enclosure remained in regular use throughout much of the Iron Age. Perhaps this entrance was 'decommissioned' in order to strengthen the line of the defences, restricting access to just one point along the enclosure circuit. However, we are well aware of the way in which practical action in the Iron Age was heavily structured by and served to reproduce cosmological principles (e.g. Giles & Parker Pearson 1999). This extended to the orientation of roundhouse doorways and enclosure entrances, these showing a preference towards the east or south-east (Hill 1995, fig. 8.7; Oswald 1997). At the risk of generalization, there is reason to believe the east was commonly regarded as auspicious and the west as inauspicious, marginal or related to potentially dangerous states. While many hillforts possessed paired western and eastern entrances throughout their functional lives, there are a number that display a similar sequence to that revealed at Lodge Hill, with western gateways being blocked at an early stage. Examples include Danebury (Hampshire), Moel y Gaer (Flintshire), Yarnbury (Wiltshire) and within the region at Llanmelin (see Williams, below). Perhaps reflecting the symbolic danger associated with westerly entrances, in instances where these were retained they could sometimes become massively over-elaborated, as with the later phases at Maiden Castle, Dorset (Sharples 1991a). It remains informed speculation, but was the western entrance at Lodge Hill blocked because of a developing sense that its presence was inauspicious? At a later date this route into the hillfort was re-established, a process that involved cutting through the substantial bank at this point. When this happened is uncertain, but it could well be associated with Roman or even early post-Roman phases of activity (see below).

The sequence of development
Given that only a limited area of this large and complex monument has been excavated, only a tentative sequence of development can be offered. The earliest hillfort was most likely univallate, with a timber-framed rampart, internal quarry pits, and entrances at the eastern and western ends. On the basis of artefactual evidence, this was probably created around the 5th century BC. At some stage during the middle or late Iron Age additional circuits of defence were added, some of these with V-shaped ditches and dump ramparts (see Cunliffe 2005, 351-8, for similar sequences elsewhere). The western entrance was blocked, and the eastern probably elaborated; though the detail of the latter has been removed by the building of Lodge Farm. This process of multivallation is likely to have been complex, with various episodes of re-modelling. An indication of this complexity is provided by 'partially buried' lengths of bank and ditch visible in the north-eastern part of the site, one of which is peculiar in that it appears to 'curve off' from the line of the defences and then stop abruptly. A short length of bank between the second and third ramparts on the south-western side of the hillfort is also anomalous, and must relate to an early phase of multivallation.

The status of the small oval enclosure within the western third of the interior remains uncertain. Lacking a formal western entrance, it must come either at the beginning of the sequence (i.e. it is the original hillfort), or very late, after the reinstatement of the western entrance, which may have occurred during the late Roman or post-Roman periods. Further investigation of this earthwork is clearly desirable in order to resolve its position in the sequence of site development.

Activities and artefacts
While the number of finds recovered during the excavation is not great, a reasonable range of Iron Age material culture is present: pottery, briquetage, worked stone, small iron fittings and a brooch. Metallurgical debris is also present, though the absence of furnaces and smithing hearths need occasion no surprise since traces of such structures will rarely survive (Tim Young pers. comm.). From these the occurrence of activities such as food processing and cooking, iron-working and perhaps woodworking can be inferred. All of these are within the range of tasks normally performed at hillforts and Iron Age settlements in general.

It would be desirable to know whether the evidence for iron-working in Trench 1 was specific to this area, and perhaps contained within the small inner enclosure. This cannot be resolved without further excavation of the interior, but it is worth noting that distinct metalworking areas were often created within Iron Age sites. Hingley has observed that such activity was often located near to or on the periphery of sites, and frequently close to entrances (1997, 12), as, for example, at the Collfryn enclosure, Powys (Britnell 1989). Both symbolic and practical reasons can be offered for this (Hingley 1997, 12), which are not of course mutually exclusive. As a 'magical and impressive' act, Hingley suggests that iron-working was closely identified with complex ideas of real and symbolic regeneration (ibid.), which might explain the frequent occurrence of formal deposits in association with smithing areas. At South Cadbury, Somerset, weaponry, bucket and cauldron fragments were deposited within an area of metalworking in the southern part of the hillfort interior (Barrett *et al.* 2000, 300-1). The spread of cremated animal bone and an intact (and fastened) La Tène brooch from the area of the inner enclosure entrance

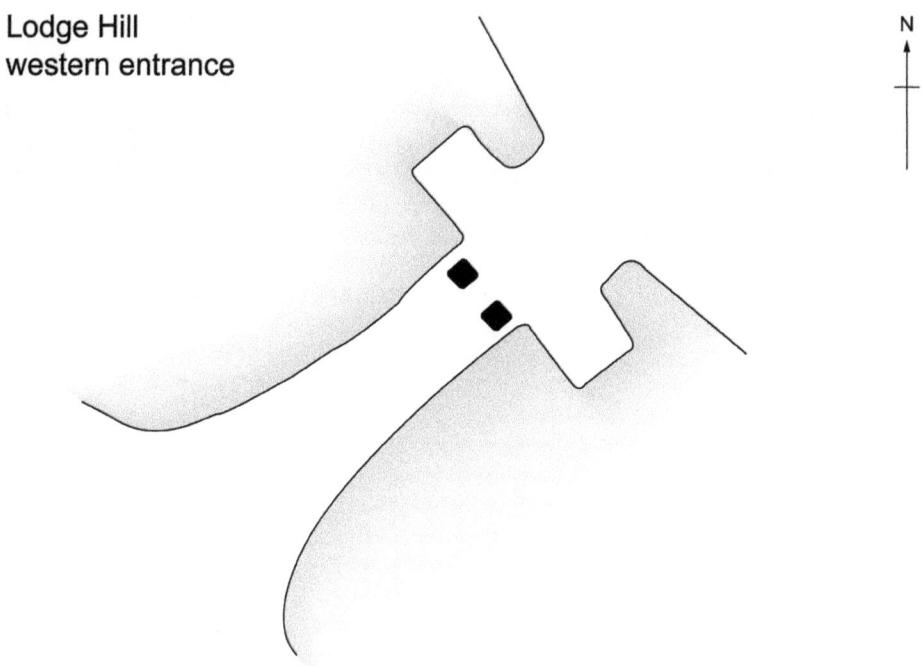

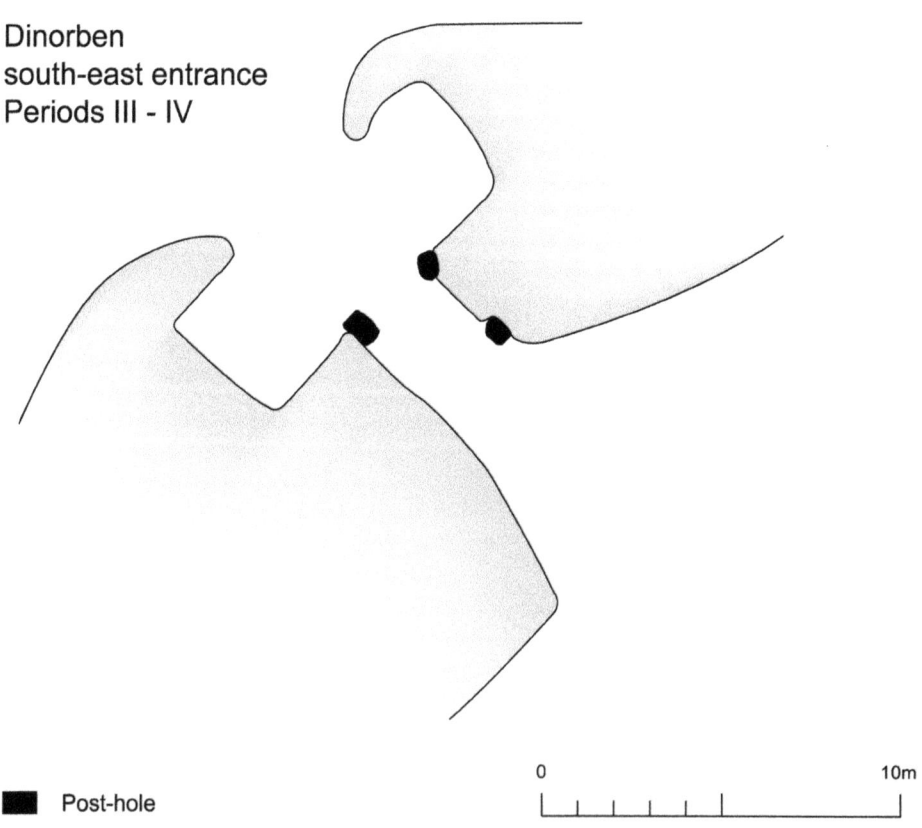

FIGURE 32. 'GUARD CHAMBER' ARRANGEMENTS AT LODGE HILL (CONJECTURAL RECONSTRUCTION BASED ON TRENCH 3 FEATURES) AND DINORBEN (AFTER GARDNER & SAVORY 1964)

at Lodge Hill could result from comparable depositional practices.

At least three of the five excavated hillforts in the county (Llanmelin, Sudbrook, Twyn y Gaer and Lodge Hill) have produced evidence for metalworking, though such activity was not restricted to hillforts, as indicated by fragments of vitrified hearth lining from Iron Age contexts at the Thornwell Farm farmstead (Starley, in Hughes 1996, 77).

The Iron Age ceramic assemblage from Lodge Hill is dominated by vessels from the Malvern region of Hereford-Worcester (Peacock 1968, Morris 1982), though there are also two sherds in what may prove to be local fabrics. The acquisition of pottery from a distant source is not in itself surprising. It fits a more general pattern for the middle-late Iron Age, where pottery production was frequently concentrated at specific locations, and ceramics exchanged on a regional scale (Morris 1994, 377; 1997). Conforming to pattern, Lodge Hill falls within Morris' western zone of the Severn Valley area where assemblages are exclusively or predominantly made-up of regionally produced pottery (Morris 1994, 378). Rather than direct trade from source, down-the-line exchange systems are implied by regression analysis, perhaps utilizing existing kinship networks (ibid.). What is remarkable about the Lodge Hill material is that it extends the known distribution of Malvernian wares for some considerable distance to the south-west, and that Severn Estuary-Bristol Channel calcite-tempered wares are absent. The latter were certainly in production by the late Iron Age, and have a wide regional distribution along the Severn Estuary and into the Vale of Glamorgan (Allen 1998). Their absence from the site may well be indicative of regional political affiliation, implying more sustained contact with communities to the north-east (via the Usk valley) than those occupying the Severn Estuary zone.

The involvement of the site in long distance exchange networks is further demonstrated by the occurrence of Droitwich salt containers. Salt production at the Droitwich springs spanned much of the Iron Age, being underway by the 6th century BC and continuing until the eve of the Roman conquest (Morris 1985). Comparable assemblages of briquetage are also known from other sites in the region, notably the hillforts of Twyn y Gaer and Sudbrook (ibid.). Given the distribution of this material, the major river valleys of the Usk and Wye would seem to have functioned as corridors along which both salt and Malvernian pottery were exchanged, the latter perhaps 'piggy-backing' off the former (Morris pers. comm.). Quite what the presence of 'imported' material at these sites implies is open to debate. While hillforts may have acting as foci for the redistribution of such goods during periodic communal gatherings, the presence of fragmented briquetage could imply consumption rather than the breaking down of salt cakes prior to redistribution to smaller-scale sites in the vicinity of hillforts. In many respects, engagement in such exchange networks was strictly unnecessary, if one takes a functional perspective, since both pottery and salt could be obtained from the working of local resources. However, this pattern of activity is widespread and, following Halstead & O'Shea (1982), Morris suggests participation in medium- and long-distance exchange served as a form of 'social storage', maintaining social bonds in order to facilitate inter-group assistance in times of need (harvest failure, warfare and so forth)(Morris 1997).

Economies and taskscapes
Charcoals recovered from the phase 1 and 2 deposits within Trench 1 include a diverse range of wood species, probably sourced from a variety of locations within the surrounding landscape. Oak is, unsurprisingly, dominant, and would have been employed in quantity for the construction of interior buildings and the framing of the rampart and gateways. It is difficult to extrapolate from the limited area investigated just how much timber would have been required, but the demands of this and other hillforts in the region must have significantly depleted adjacent woodland, leaving as marked a scar on the landscape as the enclosures themselves. As Ruth Young has stressed, oak and coppiced hazel, from managed woodland, also provided an important fuel for iron-working; while the presence of gorse could either indicate clearance or selective use for specialized rites (here linked with a possible animal cremation). Alder, present in small quantities, is representative of carr woodland, perhaps fringing low-lying areas of the Usk floodplain or the Severn Estuary. Its presence is a reminder of the rhythms of productive activity, which would have seen people move from the elevated locale of the hillfort onto the surrounding lowlands on a routine basis.

Cereal production is hardly evidenced at all, with only a single grain of wheat (*Triticum* sp.) from an early context within the interior. This may be as much a reflection of survival as anything else, though the absence of querns is also telling. Perhaps activities within the site were markedly spatially segregated, with occupation *per se* and food preparation and consumption taking place in the more open eastern two-thirds of the hillfort. Even if the status of cereals remains ambiguous, livestock would have formed an important component of the economy of the hillfort's occupants: providing meat for routine consumption, feasting and gift-giving, and secondary products such as milk, wool, skins and so forth. Unfortunately, the acidity of the soil meant that only calcined animal bone survived. Sheep and chicken were identified, with bones of the former and/or other medium-sized mammals predominant. Faunal assemblages from broadly contemporary sites in the region, such as Thornwell Farm, Llanmelin, and Goldcliff on the Gwent Levels, include the usual range of domesticates – cattle, sheep/goat and pig – along with some horse and red deer (Nash-Williams 1933, Hughes 1996, Bell *et al.* 2000). A mixed and perhaps flexible agricultural economy is implied.

5.2. Lodge Hill in its regional context

Situating Lodge Hill within a regional Iron Age sequence is difficult, not least because so few Iron Age sites in Gwent have been subject to recent detailed investigation. Notable work has been undertaken by Martin Bell and others on the foreshore of Severn Estuary to the east of Newport at Goldcliff (Bell *et al.* 2000), leading to the recovery of important environmental data, and a remarkable range of structures related to seasonal exploitation of the Levels during the Iron Age. Development-led excavations at Thornwell Farm, near Chepstow (Hughes 1996), and Portskewett (Clarke 1999) have provided insight into non-hillfort, dryland settlement, which otherwise remains poorly attested in the region. Contrast might be made between the fine-grained, high-quality data available from wetland sites on the southern edge of the region, and (because of less favourable preservation) the more coarse-grained and impoverished material and environmental assemblages from much of the Usk valley and Gwent uplands.

The most visible Iron Age archaeology remains that of hillforts, of which Children and Nash list 43 examples in Gwent (1996, 87). These form a 'network' along the major river valleys of the Usk and Wye, along the coastal zone in the south and the edge of the Black Mountains in the north. By comparison with those in central southern and south-western England, or further north along the Welsh borders, these sites are small, with all but one under 6ha (Howell & Pollard 2004). Both univallate and multivallate, with wide- and close-spaced ramparts, with and without internal sub-divisions, and different configurations of entrance, they display a notable degree of morphological variation. With this may come variability in chronology, intended role and function. There is certainly no need to see these enclosures as part of a unified 'system' of settlement.

With Lodge Hill included in the list, only five Gwent hillforts have been the subject of excavation on any meaningful scale (Fig. 33). Llanmelin and Sudbrook in the south of the county were investigated by trenching before the Second World War (Nash-Williams 1933, 1939). Twyn y Gaer on the edge of the Black Mountains was the focus for a concerted campaign of work in the late 1960s and early 1970s, but only an interim report is available (Probert 1976). Coed y Bwnydd, overlooking the Usk valley, was dug at a similar time, and the results of this work were fully reported (Babbidge 1977). With such a small sample of investigated sites it would be premature to outline a developmental sequence in a way that has been possible for other regions (e.g. Cunliffe 1984). Tentatively, the main phase of hillfort construction might be placed broadly concurrent with sites such as Croft Ambrey and Midsummer Hill in the Welsh Borders, dating to the 6th and 5th centuries BC (Lynch *et al.* 2000, 152). Belonging to the last two centuries BC, Sudbrook is a notable exception. In the following section, a summary review is provided of each of these excavated hillforts.

Llanmelin

This multivallate hillfort with two, and in places three, banks and ditches is located 2km NNW of Caerwent, the site of the Romano-British *civitas* capital of the Silures, and overlooks the Severn estuary (Nash-Williams 1933). A single entrance is located to the south-east with the most substantial defences on the north-east of the site. The enclosed area at Llanmelin is 2.3ha. There are several interesting features outside the main hillfort defences including a distinctive series of three sub-rectangular enclosures and an additional length of bank and ditch (the Annexe) appended to the hillfort on the south-east, and a small earthwork enclosure known as 'the Outpost' 250m to the north-east. In keeping with the excavation techniques of the time, in the investigation of the site in the early 1930s, narrow trenching was employed. As a geophysical survey undertaken during 2003 has demonstrated (Williams, Appendix 1), traces of roundhouses and other smaller structures were in consequence missed.

Recent geophysical and earthwork survey suggests a complex sequence of development. The hillfort began as a univallate enclosure with a stone revetted bank and entrances at the west and south, perhaps constructed during the 4th or 3rd centuries BC. Occupation material later sealed by the banks of the Annexe indicates extra-mural settlement during an early phase. Probably in the 2nd century BC, the hillfort was redefined by the construction of a multivallate enclosure with *glacis* style defences and an in-turned entrance to the south. The entrance banks were stone-faced and topped with a timber platform and palisade (Nash-Williams 1933, 279). The enclosures forming the Annexe were probably constructed late in the Iron Age. The Outpost, on the other hand, appears to have been an early feature, probably belonging to the first hillfort phase.

Trenching of the interior during the 1930s produced some evidence relating to occupation; and that has been corroborated by the discovery of several roundhouse gullies in a recent geophysical survey (Appendix 1). There was evidence of metalworking in the form of a clay crucible with fused copper alloy slag. The pottery includes simple and bead-rim jars with limestone fabrics as well as a few Glastonbury-style vessels. There were more decorated vessels at Llanmelin than at Lodge Hill or Sudbrook. Fragmentary 'knobbed and ribbed' copper alloy bracelets, perhaps La Tène I or II (Cunliffe 2005, 470-1) were found in the innermost ditch of the hillfort (Nash-Williams 1933, fig. 54). Faunal remains recovered from Iron Age contexts include cattle, sheep/goat, pig and horse, and may indicate a fairly typical mixed economy (Cowley, in Nash-Williams 1933, 310).

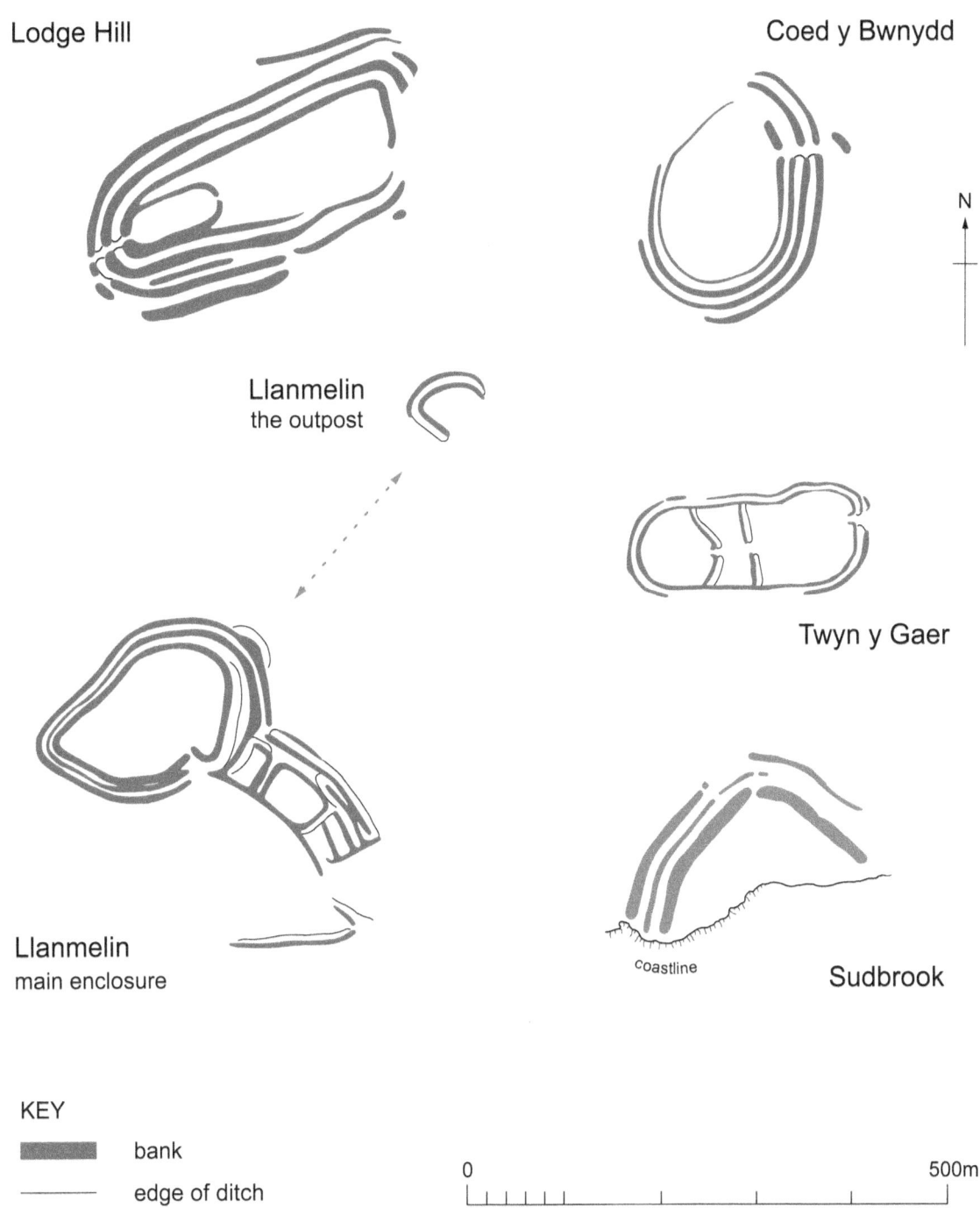

FIGURE 33. EXCAVATED GWENT HILLFORTS

As has been seen, the Annexe was a late addition to the hillfort. The enclosures making up this feature are frequently explained as animal pens, but they are unusual in that two have no apparent entrances and there was little evidence for occupation within them. The incomplete skeletons of an adult male and adult female were associated with enclosures A and B (Nash-Williams 1933, 310), though it is uncertain if these date to the Iron Age. The enclosures are morphologically similar to contemporary (i.e. 1st century BC/AD) enclosures associated with cremation burials in the south-east of England, such as those at King Harry Lane, St. Albans (Stead & Rigby 1989), and recently excavated at Stanway, Colchester (Crummy 2002). It is tempting to link the finds of human bone with the known mortuary function of superficially similar contemporary sites, and suggest that the Annexe served as a series of funerary enclosures. Another unusual feature of Llanmelin is the presence of additional lengths of bank and ditch to the east of the hillfort. These swing around on the north and south in such a way as to 'enclose' the Annexe. These features are essentially undated and Nash-Williams thought that they might be medieval (1933, 288). An alternative, and perhaps more convincing, interpretation would be to see them as late Iron Age and related to the dyke systems often associated with *oppida*.

Nash-Williams provided a short site chronology for Llanmelin, spanning c.200BC to AD75 (1933, 289). In fact, the earlier part of the range might be extended into the 4th century BC, making the first phase of Llanmelin broadly contemporary with the earlier phases at Lodge Hill. Both sites display a similar sequence of development, beginning as univallate enclosures with a structured bank, then becoming multivallate earthworks with *glacis*-style defences.

Sudbrook Camp
Nash-Williams (1939) also conducted excavations at Sudbrook Camp, a promontory fort on the edge of the Severn Estuary. Its location suggests a strategic placement to command the 'Old Passage' crossing the estuary between Portskewett and Aust (Whittle 1992, 49). The multivallate defences consist of a massive inner bank and two further lines of bank and ditch with a counterscarp bank beyond. The outer banks are of simple 'dump' construction, with no evidence of stone or timber revetment. The inner bank, which rises up to 4.9m high, was thought by the excavator to be of four construction phases (Nash-Williams 1939, 45-7), although perhaps only two phases are represented, both fronted by stone walling revetment. The broad V-shaped ditches at Sudbrook show no signs of re-cutting. It should be noted that there was evidence of pre-bank occupation associated with middle Iron Age pottery as well as cattle, sheep/goat and pig bone (Nash-Williams 1939, 47).

Occupation deposits were found within quarry hollows behind the inner rampart. These included stratified artificial surfaces interpreted as floors, the lower of which produced querns and animal bone. Middle and late Iron Age pottery was found, including calcite-tempered bead-rim jars and Glastonbury-style vessels; little of this material was decorated (Nash-Williams 1939, 50). Nine brooches, including Colchester and Colchester derivative brooches of the 1st century AD were recovered. Droitwich briquetage was also present (Morris 1985, table 1). A similar assemblage, with quantities of bead-rimmed calcite-tempered pottery, a penannular and a La Tène I brooch and briquetage, was recently found in the backfill of a ditch at nearby Portskewett (Clarke 1999). There was evidence for glass and iron-working including slag and clinker at Sudbrook (Nash-Williams 1939, 50). Geophysical survey suggests the presence of numerous circular and rectangular structures within the interior (Sell 2001, 123-6), probably relating to the later prehistoric and Roman occupation (Fig. 34).

The excavation of Sudbrook, like that at Llanmelin, was limited by the techniques employed in the 1930s. Nevertheless, some conclusions can be drawn. Sudbrook appears to have been a late construction with occupation probably beginning in the 2nd century BC. Large quantities of Roman material including pre-Flavian coins, as well as samian and other Roman pottery may indicate Roman military occupation in the 1st century AD; and there is reason to believe that subsequent Romano-British occupation could have been protracted.

Twyn y Gaer
Twyn y Gaer, near Llanfihangel Crucorney, is one a small group of hillforts commanding the southern approaches to the Black Mountains, others being the complex multivallate site at Pentwyn and the small enclosure on Twyn Yr Allt (Olding 2000, 93). The site was excavated in the 1960s and early 1970s, largely by volunteers from the Abergavenny Archaeological Group (Probert 1976). A final report is still awaited. The hillfort is an oval enclosure on a knoll subdivided by 'cross-banks', which create three distinct enclosures (the western encompassing 0.5ha, the central 0.3ha, and the eastern 0.9ha). The entrances face east with the main and western enclosure entrances being in-turned; the middle entrance is simple.

The excavations revealed a long and complex history of construction and occupation, beginning with an oblong enclosure with the middle 'cross-bank' at its eastern end. This was associated with a fenced 'annexe' extending to the east, the stake-lines of which had seen successive replacement. Perhaps intended as a corral for stock, this is associated with a single radiocarbon date of 400-200 cal BC (at 95.4%). On the basis of this the excavator dated the first phase of activity on the site to the 5th century BC. Subsequent expansion of the hillfort to the east resulted in the enclosure of the area of the annexe. The entrance in this phase included a stone revetted passageway and gate which underwent subsequent

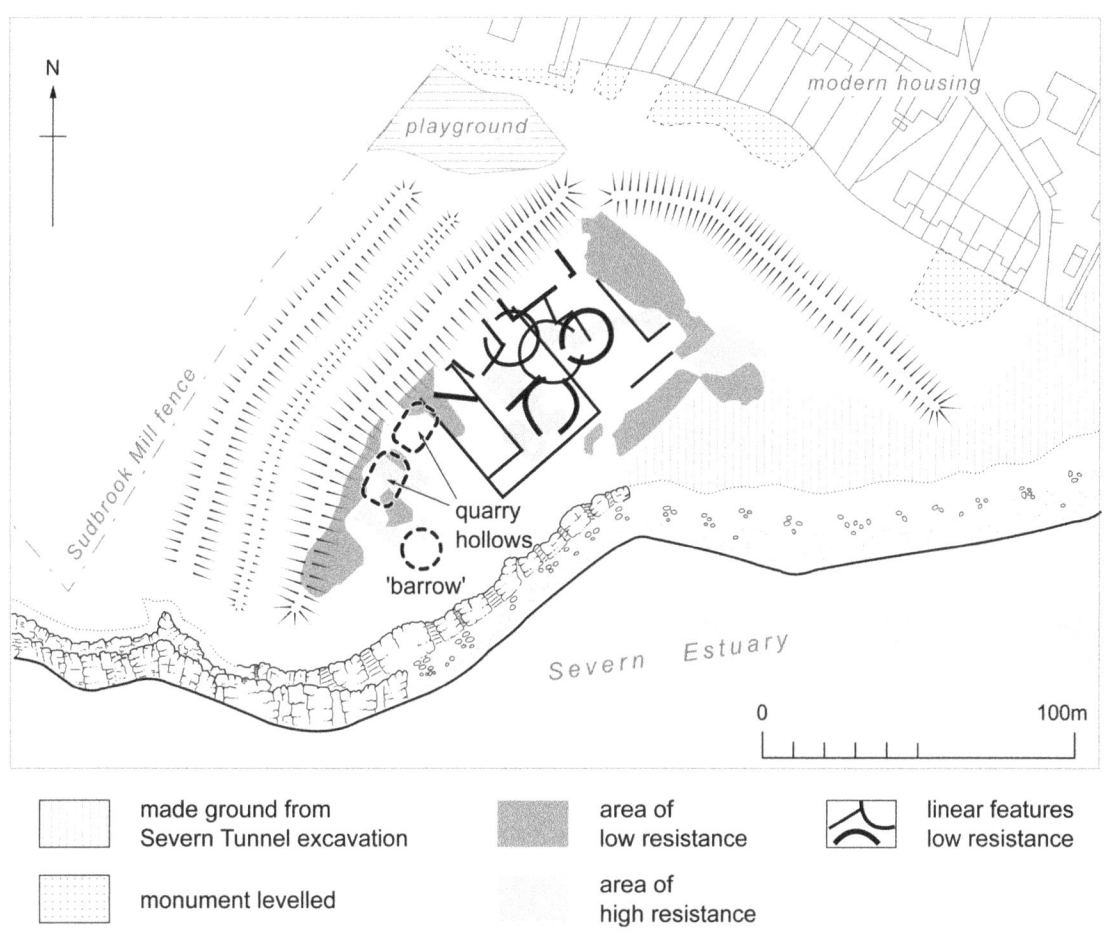

FIGURE 34. SUDBROOK CAMP. FEATURES REVEALED THROUGH EXCAVATION AND GEOPHYSICAL SURVEY (AFTER NASH-WILLIAMS 1939 AND SELL 2001)

episodes of modification, eventually becoming a narrow passage. The main rampart was stone revetted with, eventually, a stone-built rampart walk. The last phase saw construction of the western cross-bank creating a much smaller enclosure entered through an in-turned gate (Probert 1976, 109-15).

Occupation of the site was indicated by post-holes (some paired and perhaps forming roundhouse entrances), burnt daub and at least one building platform. Associated finds included pottery, metalwork, querns and iron-working debris. The limited ceramic assemblage (around five vessels) includes both Llanmelin-Lydney and Malvernian styles. Also found was Droitwich briquetage, iron and copper alloy artefacts including La Tène II brooches and glass beads (Adam Gwilt pers. comm.). The Llanmelin-Lydney sherds were associated with the final phase of occupation at Twyn y Gaer, leading the excavator to suggest that the changes, both structural and artefactual, in this phase reflected southern influences. He argued that 'there was a cultural, if not a political, extension of Silurian power into this district' (Probert 1976, 118). Caution should be exercised, since claims of 'Silurian influence' were based largely on the presence of one or two Llanmelin-Lydney style vessels. Constructing political histories from sherds alone is a tenuous exercise.

Coed y Bwnydd
Overlooking the Usk valley, Coed y Bwnydd, near Bettws Newydd, is a small hillfort enclosing an area of 1.4ha (Babbidge 1977). Excavations were undertaken in 1969-71 and were largely limited to investigating parts of the northern third of the interior and defences on the south-east, east and north-east. The hillfort is multivallate on the east and south where it fronts onto the hilltop plateau, but is reduced to a single line on its steeper western side. A straight entrance leads through the defences, but direct access is blocked by a lunate outwork. The excavator believed that the hillfort was originally bivallate (Babbidge 1977, 173).

Excavation provided evidence for re-cutting of the ditches as well as at least two phases of bank construction. There was timber revetting to the inner bank. In both the north and south of the interior post- and

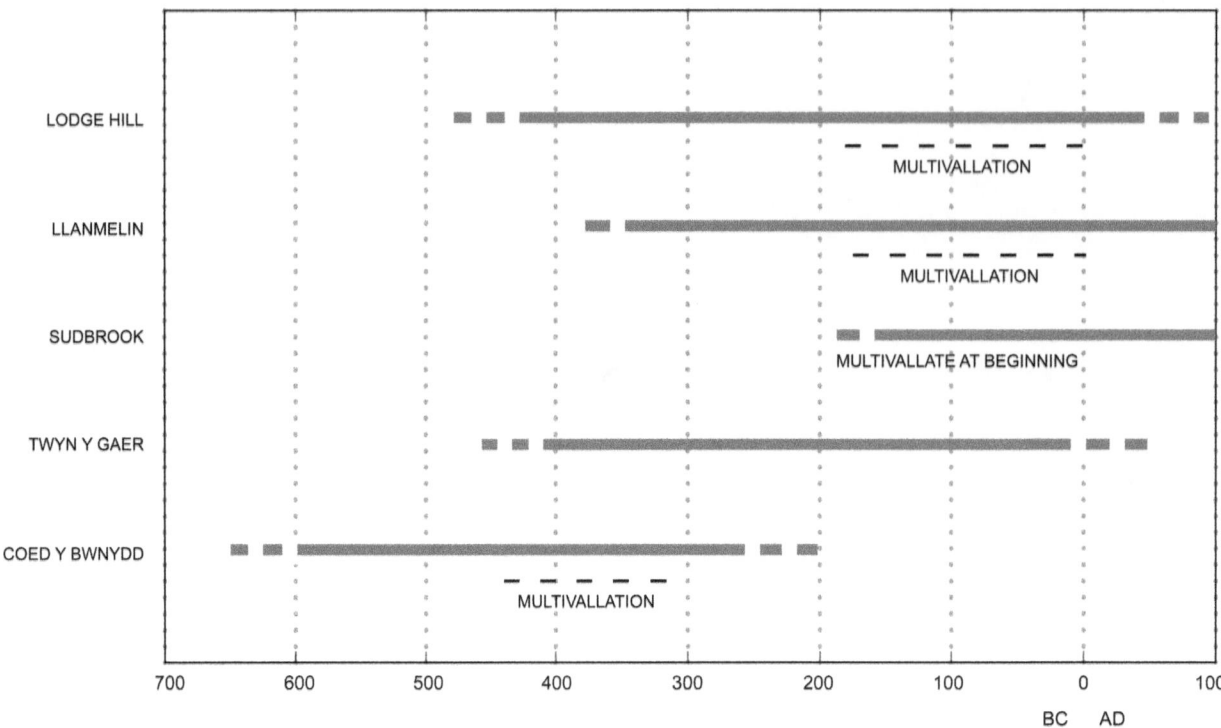

FIGURE 35. PHASES OF ACTIVITY AT EXCAVATED GWENT HILLFORTS

stake-built structures were encountered suggesting some occupation. In particular, the partial plans of four roundhouses were revealed, which were later than quarry scoops at the back of the inner rampart. Radiocarbon dates from the stake wall of one of these structures were 2390+70BP (HAR-546) and 2350+90BP (HAR-547) (Babbidge 1977, 172). These results give a calibrated range, at 95.4% probability, of 800-200BC, weighted towards 550-350BC, placing the structure in the early/middle Iron Age. Since the structure cuts the fill of the quarry hollow and replaces an earlier roundhouse, it does not represent the first phase of activity at Coed y Bwnydd.

Activity on the site seems to have ended in the 3rd century BC, so the final multivallation is early, being perhaps late 5th or early 4th century BC in date (Babbidge 1977, 177). This is interesting, and in some respects surprising, as it runs counter to the accepted pattern in which such multivallation occurs late in the Iron Age (Cunliffe 2005, 357). There is a suggestion that there was organised slighting of the defences at Coed y Bwnydd at the end of the Iron Age (Babbidge 1977, 173).

The lack of finds, even on an apparently aceramic site, is surprising, particularly the absence of metalwork and stone implements such as querns and pounders. The question must arise whether, despite evidence of structures within the interior, the site was subject to prolonged or temporary occupation. There may be parallels with the Iron Age phases at the Breiddin in Powys where the numerous roundhouses and four-post structures in the interior were originally interpreted as evidence of a thriving, almost proto-urban, settlement (Musson 1991). Recent re-assessment of the environmental evidence, however, implies that the site was little utilised and the roundhouses only briefly occupied (Buckland et al. 2001, 71). One explanation would be that activity only occurred intermittently with any short-lived presence 'encompassed within the seasonal round of exploitation of the hilltop for pasture and festivals' (ibid.).

The results of these investigations reinforce the considerable diversity implied by surface evidence: there is no 'typical' Gwent hillfort, nor shared sequences of development beyond periodic reworking of the enclosure circuits (Fig. 35). All might be seen to have produced evidence of occupation of kinds – and to this list can be added the site of Coed-y-Caerau, on the east side of the Usk opposite Caerleon, where recent geophysical survey has revealed traces of roundhouses (Mike Hamilton pers. comm.) – but this could vary from more or less permanent settlement at Llanmelin to seasonal visits at sites like Coed y Bwnydd and Twyn y Gaer. On this evidence, it would be premature to think of an organised 'system' of hillforts within the region. Rather, we have evidence of a common tradition of large enclosure construction during the mid-late 1st millennium BC, created around varied and contingent modes of communal expression and landscape occupation.

5.3. Hillforts and social relations in south-east Wales

Hillforts became dominant symbols in the Iron Age landscape, but symbols of what – military prowess, elite power, or community endeavour and belonging? As the reassessment of the Breiddin makes clear, the interpretation of these sites is rarely straight-forward. The roles of these sites can be envisaged as many and varied. Their existence may or may not be testimony to the existence of Iron Age social elites controlling the production and distribution of agricultural produce or other goods. Earlier models of marked social stratification, with control vested in chiefdoms, now look increasingly unsatisfactory. There is certainly no obvious evidence for any kind of 'elite presence' at Lodge Hill or other excavated hillforts in Gwent, unless activities such as metalworking were controlled by dominant individuals or sectional groups. Even the mobilisation of labour and resources required to construct these enclosures could be managed through a system of co-operation and communal endeavour rather than coercion from 'the top'. These may have been quite 'fluid' spaces. The size and make-up of occupying groups could well vary between hillforts, and between individual phases of single sites. Collis has outlined a range of possibilities for hillfort residence, from permanent to sporadic, and from the presence of the total population to that of age-sets or 'ethnic' groups (1981, 72). Certainly the evidence from Gwent sites, outlined above, suggests both permanent and transitory residence.

Any discussion of hillforts tends to revolve around and return to the role of their defences. This is not surprising, nor necessarily problematic, since they are the features that define these monuments, and provided the most impressive displays of constructional activity during the Iron Age. Whether the building of such elaborate defences indicated real or perceived threat, a form of display or conspicuous consumption, or the creation of bounded spaces for communal or socially 'marginal' activities (Bowden & McOmish 1987, Collis 1996, Hill 1996), we should not downplay their importance. They helped to define these sites as special places and, as Hill suggests, different from non-hillforts as *not-farmsteads* (Hill 1996, 108). As such, they could carry enormous symbolic significance as potent boundaries defining separate zones of social space, time and identity. Their reworking added a sense of time-depth and laboured connections between past and present. Through piecemeal addition of extra lines of rampart and ditch, multivallation could come to stand as much as a record of long-term commitment, solidarity and belonging to a place as a powerful statement of prestige and protection.

Iron Age hillfort ramparts were often very impressive structures, and those on Lodge Hill would have been no exception. Whether a series of stepped stone faces supported by timbers, or a vertical timber face supported by stone, the ramparts of the inner bank would have appeared very striking indeed, and would have had obvious defensive value. However, the nature and extent of warfare in the British Iron Age is poorly understood, and is still contentious (e.g. Haselgrove 1992, Sharples 1991b). As well as serving defensive functions, hillfort ramparts would also have imparted clear messages about power, status and lineage to those within and outside of these communities (q.v. Collis 1996, Hingley 1990).

The politics behind the construction of the defences can only be guessed at. There would have been co-operation and competition between different groups of people building the ramparts, whether these were appointed work gangs, or based on family or kinship units. Co-ordinating this work may have been a matter of discussion and debate amongst the communities involved, or it may have been organised by some emerging centralised authority. The tensions and negotiations involved in planning and implementing the different stages of construction would have been as complex as the architecture of the banks themselves.

The banks thus preserved in earth and stone a series of contradictions. They appeared to be final, 'solid' entities, single indisputable artefacts. And yet, they were also the product of countless indivisible social episodes, of a rich, organic interweaving of personal labour and community effort, of individual thought and centralised or community-based ideas and ideals. The people who laboured on the building of these ramparts were setting their embodied experiences of 'lived towards death' time towards a construction that they may well have known would last longer than their own lives. Conversely, the efforts and effects of this negotiated labour may have been more long lasting than the 'final' form of the architecture. Once disparate, scattered communities may have been brought together through this work, or alternatively, the social tensions set into effect during the construction may have extended divisions within an existing community. The powerful effect of this place in the landscape, as a site of construction, and as the repository of people's efforts, should not be underestimated. Explaining all this human drama and emotion as merely the result of coercive authority on the part of some 'tribal chief' would surely be too simplistic and naïve. The Lodge Hill ramparts were therefore both multivallate and multivalent structures.

5.4. The hillfort's relationship to the Legionary fortress

The establishment of the fortress of Legio II Augusta at Caerleon in the mid-70s AD brought Lodge Hill within its *territorium*, or military controlled area (Manning 2004, 190). It is uncertain whether the hillfort was occupied on any scale at this point in time, or if it had already been abandoned. Certainly events in the mid-1st century AD would have had a profound effect on traditional practices and patterns of activity, including the character of settlement. If the account provided by Tacitus in his *Annals* is to be believed, the Roman conquest of the region was far from straight-forward, with concerted resistance to Roman expansion coming from the local tribal group, the Silures, in the late 40s-early 50s. Perhaps a coalescence of originally disparate kin groups, the creation of the Silures could well have come about in the mid 1st century AD in direct response to the presence of an expansionist state-level power (cf. Wells 2001, 31-2). It might be imagined that the network of hillforts along the Usk valley played an important part in local resistance to the Roman army. However, given the effectiveness of Roman siege techniques, it is reasonable to assume that the attritional campaign waged by the Silures was maintained through guerilla warfare, in which hillforts played little if any role. In this context, while there is the possibility that the bank collapse recorded in Trench 2 at Lodge Hill results from deliberate slighting by the Roman army (see above), this need not have been as a result of an offensive measure. Other possibilities present themselves, including the later use of the hillfort by the Roman army for artillery and siege practice, or deliberate destruction occasioned by the site's status as an important symbol of earlier forms of political authority.

By the early 2nd century AD an extensive civilian settlement (*canabae*) had grown up around the Legionary fortress, and, as a place of congregation and activity of various kinds, the latter perhaps took on some of the roles previously ascribed to the hillfort – as a locus of identity, and symbol of social and political order. Extensive traces of civilian settlement have been found on three sides of the fortress (the south-west, south-east and north-east), while to the north-west, in the direction of Lodge Hill, there are extensive areas of cemetery (Evans & Maynard 1997; Brewer 2004, 209-10). By the late 2nd and 3rd centuries AD visits to the hillfort from the fortress and civilian settlement involved a journey through the resting place of the dead, contributing to an increasing sense of temporal distance and maybe otherworldliness between the two sites.

5.5. Lodge Hill and hillfort re-occupation in south-east Wales during the late Roman/early medieval period

An important aspect of excavation at Lodge Hill Camp is evidence of possible re-occupation of the site. The small oval inner enclosure within the hillfort may have been a late addition and, as has been noted above, excavation within the enclosure revealed a series of narrow terraces and post-hole settings with a small but potentially significant assemblage of late Roman pottery associated. Several sherds were highly abraded and the preponderance date from 3rd to late 4th century. Possibly related to these findings is evidence from the excavation through the inner bank and ditch which demonstrated a stone-revetted timber-laced rampart and a large collapse deposit of stone rubble which may suggest deliberate slighting. Significantly, a second phase survived as a thin rubble spread overlying soil which had formed after the collapse of the primary rampart. Three small fragments of Roman pottery including one samian sherd were recovered in the ditch fill and presumably relate to the collapse deposit or later activity. Excavation of the entrance to the hillfort demonstrated that it had been re-cut late in the history of the site. As no finds were associated, it seems appropriate to assign this recutting to a materially impoverished phase which may also point to re-occupation in the late Roman/post-Roman period. While not conclusive, this combined evidence does point strongly to re-occupation. If this is the case, it could be argued that Lodge Hill fits in well with a pattern of hillfort re-use and/or continuity in Romano-British South Wales.

Roman pottery has been found on a number of hillfort sites in Glamorgan (RCAHMW 1976, 8). In general, assemblages have been small but in several instances sherds have been recovered from primary deposits and in one, Llwynheiernin near Llansamlet, Roman material was incorporated into the rampart. This small (0.25ha) site produced two 2nd century samian sherds sealed beneath an inner bank (RCAHMW 1976, 32). Two other small Gower promontory forts, excavated by Audrey Williams in 1939, produced Roman material from apparently primary deposits. Finds at Bishopston Valley included a penannular brooch which stylistically appears to be Roman in date and a single sherd of plain samian ware recovered in the 'entrance passage' of the fort (Williams 1940). A rim sherd of a mortarium with red fabric was found on the floor surface of one of three excavated structures at High Pennard (Penard). Also associated was a single fragment of bluish green glass; a perforated disc of possible black burnished ware had been made into a spindle whorl (Williams 1941).

A particularly interesting Glamorgan site is Caer Dynnaf near Llanblethian only approximately one kilometre southwest of the Roman small town *Bovium*, modern Cowbridge. Here Roman period settlement within the enclosure took the form of half a dozen contiguous farmsteads defined by walls. The associated Romano-British pottery dates from the 1st to 4th centuries (Davies 1967b, 77-8). A similar date range is indicated at Porthkerry Bulwarks where excavation revealed three successive rectilinear buildings within a trapezoidal enclosure. The first phase was undated but the second was 1st to 2nd century AD and the third was 3rd to 4th century in date (RCAHMW 1976, 41-2). Also indicative of a long sequence of occupation through much of the Romano-British period was Cae Summerhouse near Tythegston. On this site, a small (0.2ha) almost square inner enclosure was placed within a larger (0.9ha) trapezoidal enclosure. Excavation suggested three pre-Roman phases with at least two Romano-British phases. Ceramics associated with the later occupation dated from the 2nd to 4th century (Davies 1967a, 75-7). The flanged rim of a Romano-British grey ware bowl was recovered from a 'rabbit scrape' in the ditch at the Burry Holms promontory fort (Williams 1939, 29).

On some Glamorgan sites, the evidence for Romano-British occupation is enigmatic. 'Fragments of Roman pottery' were reported in the enclosure at Caerau, Ely. Similarly, 'a few scraps' of unstratified Roman pottery were found at Castle Ditches east of Llancarfan with 'about a dozen more' collected from the ploughed interior (RCAHM 1976, 20-1, 44). Romano-British pottery and a fragment of a rotary quern have been found at Llantrithyd House (ibid., 48-50). Rotary querns are presumably indicative of Romano-British occupation; other examples have been found at Caer Dynnaf and at Llanquian east of Cowbridge (ibid., 48-50, 61-3).

This body of evidence from Glamorgan, while limited in terms of quantity of Romano-British material recovered, is strongly suggestive that hillfort use was not uncommon. Not only is there compelling evidence of re-use of Iron Age sites, Llwynheiernin suggests that at least one small hillfort was actually built or at least significantly modified after the Roman conquest of South Wales. In some instances, this hillfort occupation appears to be late re-occupation with discontinuity during the early conquest period. In other instances, occupation may have been largely continuous and in some instances long-lived. Indeed, sites like Caer Dynnaf and Porthkerry Bulwarks seem to demonstrate occupation virtually throughout the Romano-British period.

The position in Gwent, where there is no Royal Commission survey, is much less clear and evidence for re-occupation is limited. As has been seen, the few excavations in Gwent during the second half of the 20th century included 'reconnaissance' excavations at Coed y Bwnydd on Clytha Hill overlooking the Usk valley (Babbidge 1977). The objective of this work which was undertaken in 1969-71 was limited sampling to establish the potential of the site. Largely on the basis of comparative analogy with Croft Ambrey in Herefordshire, the excavator believed that Coed y Bwnydd was abandoned in the late third century BC (ibid., 177). No Roman material was reported from the excavation. The same is true of Twyn y Gaer near Cwmyoy 6km north of Abergavenny where a long-term excavation programme began in 1965. The preliminary conclusion drawn was that there was 'no occupation later than the Iron Age' on the site (Probert 1976, 115).

While there is no evidence of re-occupation or continuity of occupation during the Roman period at either Coed y Bwnydd or Twyn y Gaer, earlier excavations have demonstrated Romano-British activity on some Gwent hillfort sites. An important example is Llanmelin located approximately 2km north of Caerwent, the *civitas* capital of the Silures. The site, an oval 1.2ha enclosure with attached rectilinear annexes and a small offset 'outpost', was excavated by V.E. Nash-Williams in 1931-2 (Nash-Williams 1933). The narrow trenching technique employed limits the conclusions which can be formed with respect to the sequence and nature of occupation on the site. Nevertheless, the pottery assemblage indicates post-conquest activity. Of the 78 sherds described by Hawkes, at least 12 were identified as Roman. Perhaps significantly, the Romano-British material was concentrated in two areas. Four sherds were found on what was described as a 'rock-surface near workshop floor'. Seven additional Romano-British sherds were found in an 'occupation-layer inside S.E. defences immediately adjacent to Entrance' (ibid., 294, 296-8). Two of these sherds described as coarse red ware (nos. 23 and 24) merit re-examination. An additional Romano-British sherd was found in the fill of an outer ditch (ibid., 303). It is clear that new open area investigations are needed at Llanmelin but the evidence currently available confirms at least limited post-conquest activity on the hillfort site.

Evidence of Romano-British occupation is even more clear at Sudbrook, a promontory fort overlooking the Bristol Channel. The site was excavated by Nash-Williams in 1934-6 (Nash-Williams 1939). Sudbrook has suffered from coastal erosion and was once much larger than the existing 1.4ha enclosed area. Excavation produced 25 sherds of Romano-British pottery excluding imported samian ware. With one exception, this material was recovered from what was described as an 'occupation-layer on upper cobbled floor' of one of two structures which were assumed to have begun as Iron Age constructions. The same contexts produced sixteen sherds of samian ware (ibid., 66-72). There was subsequent later medieval occupation on the site. Five of the Romano-British coarse ware sherds were thought to be 3rd to 4th century in date. While this material was initially dismissed as evidence of no more than occasional 'squatter' occupation (ibid., 54) it is now generally believed that there was significant and probably lengthy Roman occupation on the site (Manning 2001, 14). This view is strengthened by finds from the nearby Blackrock site where a coin sequence extends from the 40s AD to AD 376 (Trueman 1988, 10).

If Sudbrook functioned as a port, ferry terminal and, possibly, naval station during the Roman period, its role was different from that of other re-used enclosed Iron Age sites in Wales and it is important to note that any questions relating to hillfort re-occupation in Gwent are hampered by the paucity of excavation which has taken place. Nevertheless, it may be significant that when the evidence of the Lodge Hill excavation is taken into account, three of the five Gwent hillforts/promontory forts to have been excavated on any scale indicate some form of Romano-British occupation. It should be noted that limited investigation at Camp Hill, Bryngwyn also produced Romano-British sherds (Leslie 1962, 7). As a consequence, while only very preliminary conclusions can be drawn, it may prove that patterns of re-occupation in Gwent do not differ dramatically from the better attested settlement patterns in Glamorgan.

It is not clear to what, if any, extent the majority of demonstrated late Romano-British hillfort re-occupation relates to early medieval settlement patterns. The difficulty in demonstrating continuous use from the late Roman to the early medieval period has been stressed in studies of early medieval settlement (Edwards & Lane 1988, 5). While a number of the known habitation sites of the 5th to 7th centuries have produced late Romano-British artefacts, it is unclear whether these assemblages represent continuation of a late Romano-British pattern, an imitation of that pattern or simply a convenient re-use of suitable sites. It may be significant, however, that in the limited number of sites where late Roman settlement can be shown to have continued into the post-Roman period such as the occupation complexes at Graeanog and Cefn Graeanog II in Gwynedd, there is little change in form or layout (Arnold & Davies 2000, 158).

Both late Roman and early medieval settlement can be demonstrated on several sites in North Wales. Dinas Emrys in Gwynedd is a notable case in point. This hillfort, which dominates important routes through Snowdonia, was occupied during the Romano-British period with an apparently early phase indicated by ceramic evidence including a small number of samian ware sherds. A significant late Roman phase of occupation is demonstrated by a ceramic assemblage that includes 3rd/4th century mortaria. Glass fragments are thought to be late or post-Roman in date. Early medieval activity on the site is confirmed by 44 sherds from a single amphora dating from the 5th or 6th century and a ceramic roundel with a stamped chi-rho pattern (Edwards & Lane 1988, 55-7, 126-7). Romano-British activity from the late 1st or early 2nd century to the 4th century has also been demonstrated at another important site in Gwynedd, Degannwy. Early medieval activity on the site is indicated by a Bi amphora sherd; up to a dozen additional sherds may be early medieval in date but this has not been confirmed. A single glass fragment may be post-Roman (ibid., 51-3, 126). Extensive Romano-British occupation is apparent at Dinorben in Clwyd where significant amounts of samian ware as well as a range of coarse wares including mortaria appear to date from the 1st to 4th centuries (Savory 1971, 60-3). While this site was clearly important during the late Roman period, early medieval activity cannot be demonstrated with confidence (Edwards & Lane 1988, 66).

The Breiddin, an important multi-phase site in Powys, was also occupied during the Romano-British period. This site is a good example of re-occupation as pottery and coin finds suggest 2nd or 3rd century occupation continuing at least until the end of the Roman period; no early Roman material was found. At least one terrace had been extended or accentuated when Roman pottery was already present on the site and the ceramic assemblage from multiple contexts confirms activity at least into the late 4th century. Perhaps significantly, at the New Pieces settlement, a small 'camp' set some 300m from the main hillfort defences, Romano-British material and two small glass fragments which may be early post-Roman in date were recovered (Musson 1991, 65-8,192-94).

These examples, while not exhaustive, provide good evidence that some Iron Age sites were occupied/re-occupied during the Roman period and, in at least some instances, after. Given the range of post conquest hillfort occupation demonstrated, it seems a reasonable assumption that a pattern of use/re-use of enclosed upland sites was a feature, and possibly an important feature, of late Roman/early medieval society. In south Wales, there are two particularly important examples which re-enforce this view. Coygan Camp was a 1.2ha promontory fort overlooking Carmarthen Bay which was partially excavated in 1963-5 prior to destruction of the site by quarrying. Over 2000 sherds of Romano-British coarse ware sherds as well as samian sherds thought by Grace Simpson to represent some 30 different vessels indicate intensive Romano-British activity on the site. Early medieval occupation is demonstrated by a single Bi amphora sherd and five sherds of Phocaean Red Slipware. Crucibles and other artefacts may also be early medieval in date (Wainwright 1967, 134-160). It was originally thought that Roman occupation at Coygan Camp was a brief late 3rd century phenomenon. Reassessment of the ceramic assemblage by J.L. Davies, however, shows that occupation was from the late 2nd century to the late 4th century (Edwards & Lane 1988, 46). It seems likely that, at least in this case, continuity of occupation extended into the 5th century and later.

The most intensive 5th to 7th century occupation demonstrated to date in Wales is Dinas Powys, located on a limestone ridge some four miles south-west of Cardiff. The site was excavated between 1954 and 1958 (Alcock 1963). Stone-revetted banks and ditches cut off the 'neck' of the promontory and formed an enclosure within which two sub-rectangular buildings were defined by drip gullies. The impressive artefact assemblage included amounts of pottery suggesting occupation beginning in the 5th century and continuing into the 7th century. The assemblage included over 80 sherds of red slipwares, some stamped or rouletted, which originated in the eastern Mediterranean. Many are examples of Phocaean slip wares from western Asia Minor, similar to sherds found at Coygan Camp, and there are examples probably produced near Carthage (Alcock 1963, 125-130; Knight pers. comm.). In appearance, these sherds are similar to *terra sigillata*, but the fabric is very porous. Other ceramic finds include over 170 fragments of amphorae produced in the eastern Mediterranean including examples from the Phocaean region and from Syria. There were also grey wares which were probably produced in the Bordeaux region and coarse beige-coloured jars also thought to have come from western France. Glass fragments representing some 40 vessels seem to have been Anglo-Saxon products. These finds indicate not only high status occupation but also involvement in an extensive trade network leading the excavator to interpret the site as an early *llys* (Alcock 1963, 61). There are attractions to viewing Dinas Powys as a *llys*, or perhaps more accurately, a proto-*llys* and that view may be strengthened by reappraisal of animal bones from the site by Gilchrist (1988). It has been suggested that the site could have functioned as the centre of an emerging, probably fairly localised, exchange system; population decline and attendant labour shortages may have been factors stimulating new administrative systems directed from convenient centres such as hillforts during the 5th to 7th centuries. If later Irish examples offer a relevant comparison, these systems may have been governed by reciprocity bound by social obligations (Gilchrist 1988, 60-1). Other high status but undefended secular sites such as Longbury Bank near Tenby (Campbell & Lane 1993) could have served a similar function.

The emergence of administrative systems, possibly functioning in some respects like the later medieval *llysoedd*, may in part account for the use/re-use of enclosed upland sites which has been demonstrated archaeologically. Other factors may have been significant as well. It has, for example, been suggested that reoccupation of hillforts could have been an indicator of continuity of land use. With respect to Glamorgan, the Royal Commission has suggested that such reoccupation 'could be accounted for on the assumption that the larger hillforts retained some legal importance in connection with land tenure' (RCAHMW 1976, 8). This is an attractive interpretation but it seems unlikely that it would have applied in the case of Lodge Hill. Given the very close proximity of this site to the Legionary fortress at Caerleon, discontinuity in land tenure in the early post conquest period would seem to have been inevitable. Indication of re-occupation at Lodge Hill is also interesting in the context of increasing archaeological evidence that considerable activity continued at the fortress site itself in the fourth century and after. Important re-enforcement of that view comes from excavation at the 'Roman Gates' site which explored defences and barracks in the north-east of the fortress (Evans & Metcalf 1992). One of the barrack blocks in this area seems to have survived as a standing structure at least as late as the 8th century. The grave of a young woman, radiocarbon dated to AD 660-900, was neatly cut through the floor of the building with only minimal disturbance to the surrounding floor area. The implication is that the grave had been dug from floor level and the fact that there was no appreciable build-up of organic material suggests that the building was standing and roofed at the time of the inhumation. The adjacent barrack block had been dismantled but sometime after *c.*AD 350 a small round-ended building carried on posts was erected on the site. A second similar structure appears to have been built over a nearby portion of the *via vicinaria*. Both these buildings, probably early medieval in date, seem to relate to the still standing barrack block. The excavators argue that 'the need for extra buildings in a vernacular style may imply a considerable population for Caerleon' (Evans & Metcalf 1992, 54-56). It is also now known that some larger Roman structures, including the fortress baths and a central tetrapylon, survived as standing structures well into the later Middle Ages (Zienkiewicz 1986, 262-8; Zienkiewicz, pers. comm.; Howell 2000, 387-95).

Assumptions of land use discontinuity in close proximity to the Roman Legionary fortress and evidence of continuing occupation on the fortress site itself make any indication of re-occupation on Lodge Hill particularly interesting. While in some respects, the late Roman/early medieval re-occupation suggested at Lodge Hill is in keeping with a widespread pattern of hillfort re-use and/or continuity, the location of the site with respect to the fortress is unique. It is important to stress that there are considerable difficulties not only in identifying but also in defining early medieval secular sites. Even basic classification systems such as 'definite', 'possible' and 'negative' (Edwards & Lane 1988, 17) leave room for interpretation. More problematic is the case of complex systems with categories including 'potential', 'possible', 'probable', 'very probable' and 'certain' (Dark 1994, 21). The nature of the fortifications at Lodge Hill with its distinctive small inner enclosure has always indicated possible re-occupation. Recent excavation now supports that interpretation and tends to move the site into a 'probable' category. Even given widespread evidence of late Roman/early medieval use/re-use of hillfort sites, Lodge Hill's location in what must have been not only a highly Romanised but also a highly militarised zone makes suggestion of re-occupation here particularly interesting and important. It seems clear, given results of the excavations in 2000, that further investigation of re-occupation at Lodge Hill Camp must now become an integral element in developing research strategies for south-east Wales.

Appendix 1: Llanmelin Hillfort, Caerwent: geophysical and earthwork survey

Daryl Williams

Llanmelin hillfort is situated 14.5km east of the city of Newport and 6.5km west of Chepstow, on the western edge of a Carboniferous limestone spur (Geological Survey 1981). It is bounded to the south by the coastal plain, to the west by a coombe encompassing the Castrogi Brook, and is approached from the north-east along the relatively level ground of the spur. The highest point of the spur is reached at the centre of the Main Camp at 102m OD, giving commanding views over the coastal plain below and the Severn estuary 5.5km distant. The site is currently surrounded by dense woodland, partially obscuring the view in all directions, except to the south-west where the ground falls steeply. Caerwent, the Romano-British town and *civitas* capital of *Venta Silurum*, lies on the plain 2km to the south-east.

The Earthworks

The earthworks are comprised of three main elements: the Main Camp, Annexe and Outpost (Fig. 33). The Main Camp is multivallate and traverses the spur, c.230 x 150m across and enclosing an area of approximately 2.3ha. Directly south-east of the semi-in-turned main entrance is the Annexe, comprising a series of three conjoined rectilinear enclosures. These cover an area of 0.9ha, measuring 122 x 70m. Whereas the closest enclosure abuts the Main Camp it is not tied in to its earthworks, the two being separated by the latter's defences. There is no direct means of communication either between the Main Camp and the Annexe or between any of the enclosures, the only entrance being a gap of unknown date in the south-west corner of Enclosure C. This southern-most enclosure is divided in two by an internal cross-bank.

The third element comprises the Outpost, situated 250m to the north-east along the ridge. This now consists of semi-circular earthworks, but was once likely to have been a circular enclosure with multiple ditch and bank defences c.60m across.

Previous Investigation

R.E.M. Wheeler surveyed the earthworks in 1923 and produced a plan of the Main Camp, Annexe and Outpost. A programme of excavation followed in 1930, 1931 and 1932, directed by V.E. Nash-Williams of the National Museum of Wales. Nash-Williams cut two main trenches, three feet wide, across the length and breadth of the camp and Annexe. Supplementary trenches were cut through the defences at intermediary points and across the entrance, Annexe enclosures and Outpost (Nash-Williams 1933). The aim of the investigation was primarily to elucidate the techniques used in the construction of the defences, the character of the settlement within the hillfort, and the major phases of the site's history.

Within the Main Camp occupation layers were discovered immediately inside the inner defences at a number of points and either side of the main entrance. No structures were identified within the hillfort interior, which proved largely devoid of features apart from a possible area of bronze working associated with a shallow scoop (Nash-Williams 1933, 249). The narrowness of Nash-Williams' trenches would, of course, have mitigated against the discovery of small features such as post-holes and beam slots. Furthermore, the work pre-dated the widespread recognition of later prehistoric timber roundhouses which followed Gerhard Bersu's pioneering excavations at Little Woodbury, Wiltshire, in 1938-9 (Bersu 1940).

The sections through the Annexe uncovered charcoal layers interpreted as 'cooking hearths', overlain by the transverse banks between Enclosures A and B, and also between Enclosures B and C (ibid., 262-4). Little evidence of prehistoric occupation was found in the interior, but the remains of two medieval buildings were found in the ditches to either side of Enclosure A (ibid., 265-7). The skull and bones of a man 25-40 years of age were recovered from the south-western ditch of Enclosure A, while the remains of an adult woman were found scattered on the rock surface to the north-east of Enclosure B.

The 2003 Survey

The survey work undertaken during the summer of 2003 was intended to build upon the work carried out by Wheeler and Nash-Williams by seeking to identify features for further investigation. To this end, the earthworks were surveyed and a geophysical survey conducted. Due to time constraints, the decision was made to limit both the topographical and geophysical survey to the area of the Main Camp. Extremely dense vegetation further limited the extent of the geophysical survey, preventing its completion towards the extremities of the camp.

Topographical Survey

Methodology

The survey was carried out using a Topcon GTS-212 EDM with readings taken along the earthworks and changes of slope within the interior of the Main Camp. These readings were then plotted and a 1:1000 scale plan produced (Fig. 36).

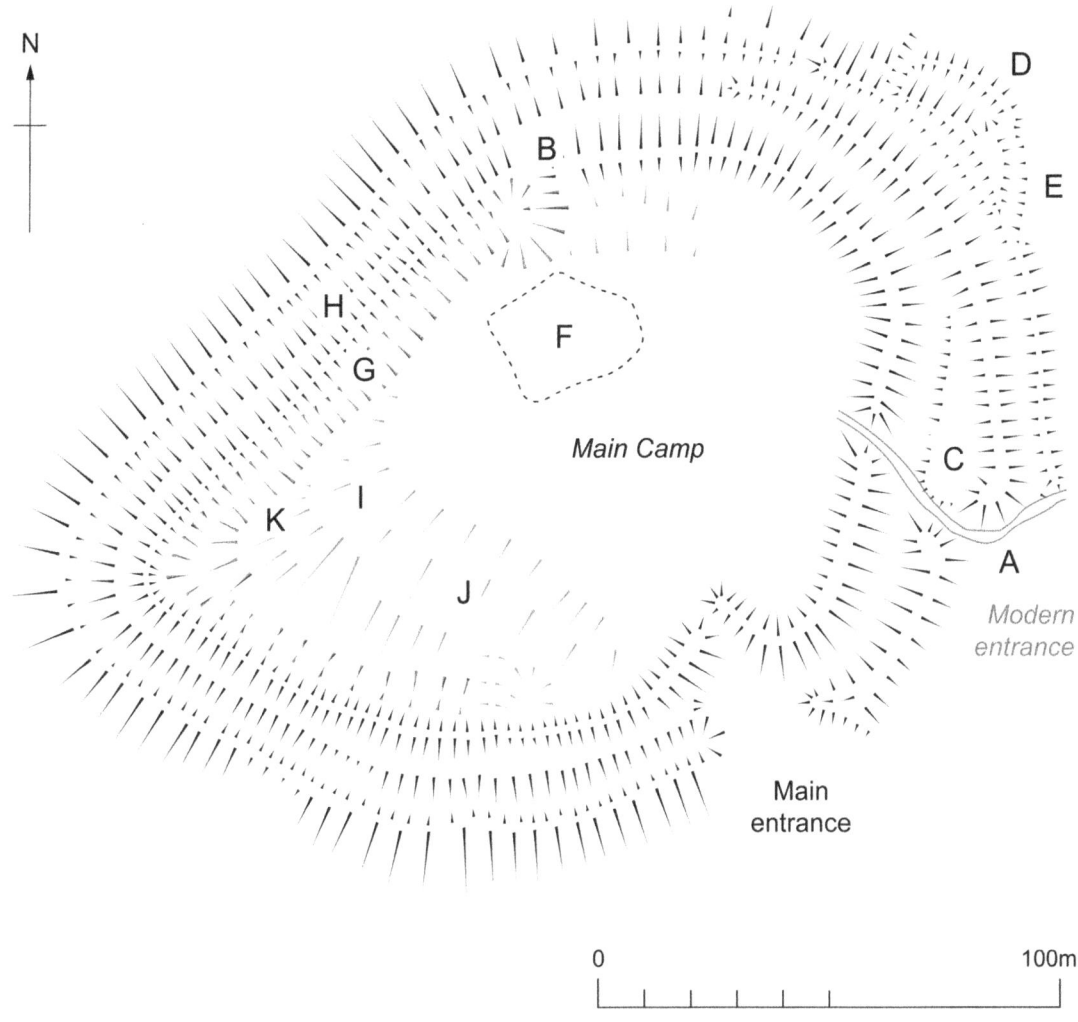

FIGURE 36. LLANMELIN. EARTHWORK SURVEY

Results
It is not intended to provide a detailed description of the earthworks here, as this can be found elsewhere (Nash-Williams 1933). A number of the interesting and/or previously unrecognised features are, however, described here.

Feature A is considered to be a modern entrance through the outer bank. The bank on either side of the entrance curves inward towards the Main Camp with the northern bank offset to the east. The ground is almost level through the outer bank but the path rises sharply through the inner bank before dropping into the camp interior.

Although thought to be a modern cut, the shape of the earthworks forming the entrance are very reminiscent of the horned earthworks forming the entrance to many other hillforts. It is known from the Nash-Williams' excavations that the outer ditch once continued across the existing main entrance of the hillfort and under the bank of the Annexe, suggesting that an earlier entrance existed somewhere around its circuit (Nash-Williams 1933, 275)(Fig. 37). It is possible, therefore, that this 'modern' entrance was forced through at the point of an earlier entrance, though this can only be confirmed by excavation.

Feature B is an anomaly in the line of the inner bank. As can be seen from the plan (Fig. 36), the bank approaches point B from the east then appears to stop, while the length of bank approaching from the south-west is considerably lower in height and joins the other bank in an offset manner. The misalignment of the bank and difference in height on either side suggest two phases of construction, or at least a substantial re-modelling of the defences.

Feature C is an area of level ground situated between the inner ditch and middle bank, adjacent to Feature A. It measures c.35m in length and is 10m wide at its southern

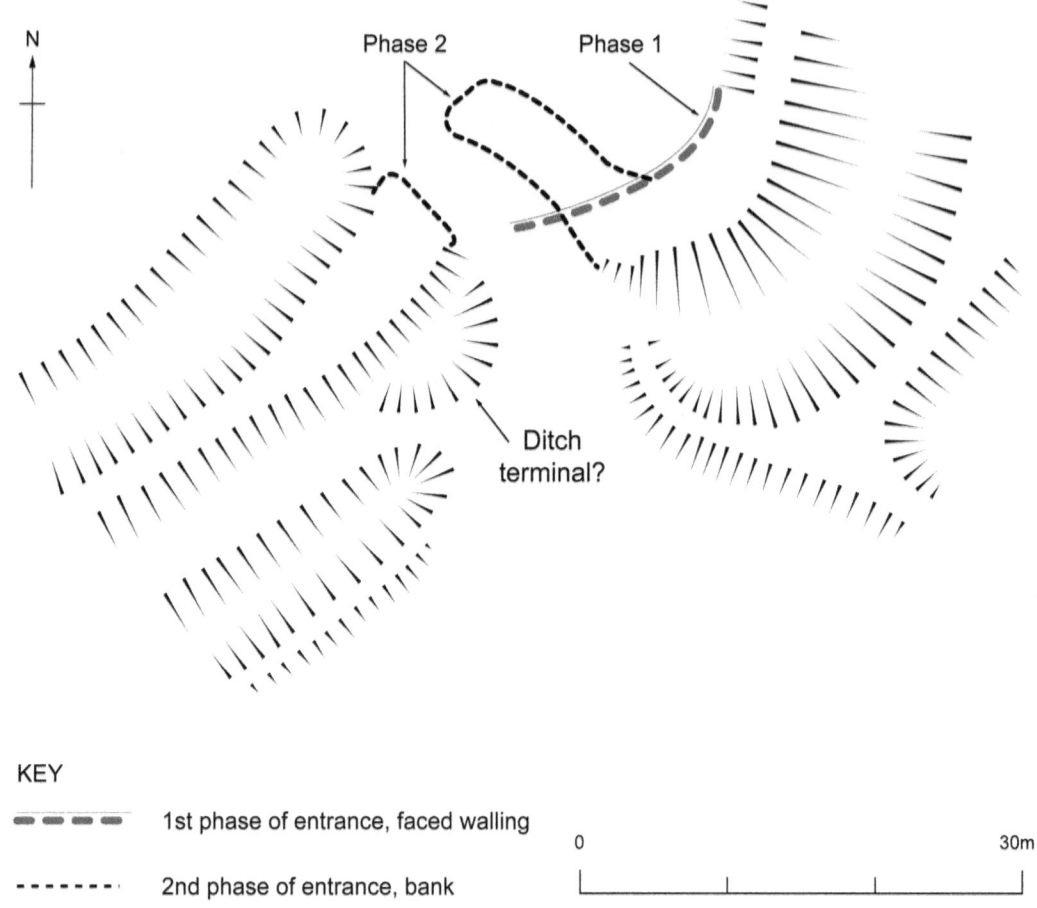

FIGURE 37. LLANMELIN MAIN ENTRANCE. EVIDENCE OF PHASING (AFTER NASH-WILLIAMS 1939)

end, tapering to a point at the north. The presence of this 'relict' area of ground may indicate a chronological separation between the inner and outer defences.

Feature D comprises a small outer bank up to 1.5m high situated outside the north-eastern circuit of the Main Camp defences. The alignment of the feature mimics the line of the inner defences for c.20m, before turning in sharply towards the camp at its southern end. It may represent part of the circuit of an earlier enclosure.

Feature E is a ditch that follows the south-eastern edge of Feature D. It is blocked at its western end by a slope rising gently to the south-west until the top of the bank is reached. Its opposite end is overlain by the small outer bank (Feature D), but continues on the other side until the main outer ditch is reached. This may represent the earliest phase of the defences.

Feature F is a slightly raised area of thick lush grass, c.30 x 20m, where the soil remains moist, even in the height of summer when the surrounding ground is dry and hard. Perhaps an in-filled pond, this area now stands a few centimetres proud of the surrounding ground surface. There is no corresponding anomaly on the geophysical survey plot.

Feature G is a curve in the inner edge of the quarry ditch on its north-western side. It corresponds with the top of the slope between the level ground of the interior to the north-east and the sloping ground to the south-west. This and Feature H may result from a phase of re-modelling of the defences.

Feature H is a curve in the bank that mirrors Feature G. At this point the bank also decreases in height to the south-west and the level berm between the bank and ditch all but disappears for c.40m.

Feature I appears to be a platform, c.15 x 10m, bordered by the quarry ditch to the north-west, and situated just below the crest of the ridge. Perhaps a building platform or a flattened length of early-phase bank and ditch.

Feature J is a gently sloping area, 10-12m in width, running north-west to south-east across the Main Camp, just below its horizon, before turning towards the entrance. The south-eastern edge is marked by a small bank a few centimetres high and c.1m wide. The slope may simply reflect the natural topography or, like Feature I, a flattened length of early-phase bank and ditch.

Feature K is a kink in the inner edge of the quarry ditch. This appears to follow the line provided by the bottom edge of Feature J and may, therefore, reflect the presence of an earlier phase of enclosure.

Geophysical Survey

The decision was made to carry out a fluxgate gradiometer survey of the site, as this survey method was particularly suited to the Carboniferous limestone geology (Clark 1996, 92). The relative absence of overhead or underground power lines and modern iron objects near the site also added to the suitability of this method.

Methodology
The survey area was divided into twenty-two 20m² grids. Readings were taken every 0.5m on a series of traverses spaced at intervals of 1m, giving a total of 800 readings per grid. The survey was carried out using a Geoscan FM36 and the results processed using Geoplot 2 and 3 software. Due to the presence of extremely dense vegetation, the survey could not encompass the edges of the hillfort interior.

Results
The results obtained from the survey (Fig. 38) display a number of well-defined features that are described below. The trenches dug in the early 1930s by Nash-Williams can be seen clearly as white anomalies across the axis of the main camp. These were not backfilled following the excavation, and it is evident that not all the trenches were reported in the 1933 publication.

Feature 1 appears to be a disturbed area covering c.25 x 40m in the most northern corner of the hillfort. The southern edge of this appears to align with the course of the small outer bank (Feature D) after it turns towards the Main Camp. It is possible this represents the interior of an early phase of enclosure.

Features 2a and 2b comprise parallel anomalies c.11m apart, running east to west from the inner bank for c.18m and 40m respectively, before making a slight angled turn towards the north-west and continuing for a further 15m. Both anomalies are likely to represent ditches, and appear to be overlain by the inner bank at their eastern end. At their western end they appear to align with Feature B.

Feature 3 is a strong linear anomaly, almost certainly a ditch, which runs for c.50m on a similar but slightly divergent trajectory to Feature 2b.

Feature 4 is a rectilinear anomaly, c. 25 x 15m with curving corners, situated in the northern part of the interior. Its northern end lies outside of survey area. It is possible that a parallel anomaly exists 3m distant from the first (seen on the south corner), although this is less well defined. The feature would appear to be a rectilinear ditched enclosure. It is not certain whether it extends beneath the inner hillfort bank or abuts it, making its position within the sequence of construction difficult to determine.

Feature 5 comprises a pair of linear anomalies extending c.4-5m in from the main entrance and appearing to make a southerly return on either side. It is possible that they mark the lines of foundation trenches for palisades, or posts to hold a combined palisade and platform around the entrance, as alluded to by Nash-Williams (1933, 279).

Features 6 and 8-22 comprise circular, semi-circular and elliptical anomalies distributed across the interior of the hillfort. They range in size from c.5-22m across and show with varying degrees of resolution. The smaller circular features with diameters of less than 15m (e.g. 9, 11, 20) are likely to represent roundhouse drip gullies, while the larger and more elliptical features could be small enclosures/compounds (e.g. 6, 15, 18).

Feature 15 must have been cut through by a trench during Nash-Williams' excavations, although he failed to recognise any structural features in this location. A deposit of occupation material, which included debris from bronze working, was found in a depression c.5m in diameter, sited 23.5m from the edge of the quarry ditch (Nash-Williams 1933, 249). This may correspond with Feature 15, although the latter appears too large at 12m in diameter and be too far into the camp to be the area mentioned. The position of Feature 18 also correlates with an occupation layer recorded by Nash-Williams (ibid.).

Feature 7 is a slightly curving or angled arrangement of anomalies, perhaps from conjoined pits or a gully.

Feature 23 consists of a pair of parallel linear anomalies c.5m apart that spring from the curve in the quarry ditch at Feature G. They run from the quarry ditch edge in a southerly direction for c.20m before terminating against a short linear anomaly.

Feature 24 is a substantial linear anomaly that follows the shallow slope (J) for c.25m before turning north-west for a further 10m and ending in a hook-shaped terminal. If continuing to the east it would run under the in-turned western bank of the main entrance and would join with a pit (ditch butt?) discovered by Nash-Williams (1933, 276). Although Nash-Williams believed this pit to be a blocking device across the berm between the inner bank and ditch, this seems an unlikely arrangement, and the feature would appear to run under the bank. If the pit and Feature 24 can be joined, the presence of an earlier and much simpler entrance can be postulated. This is given

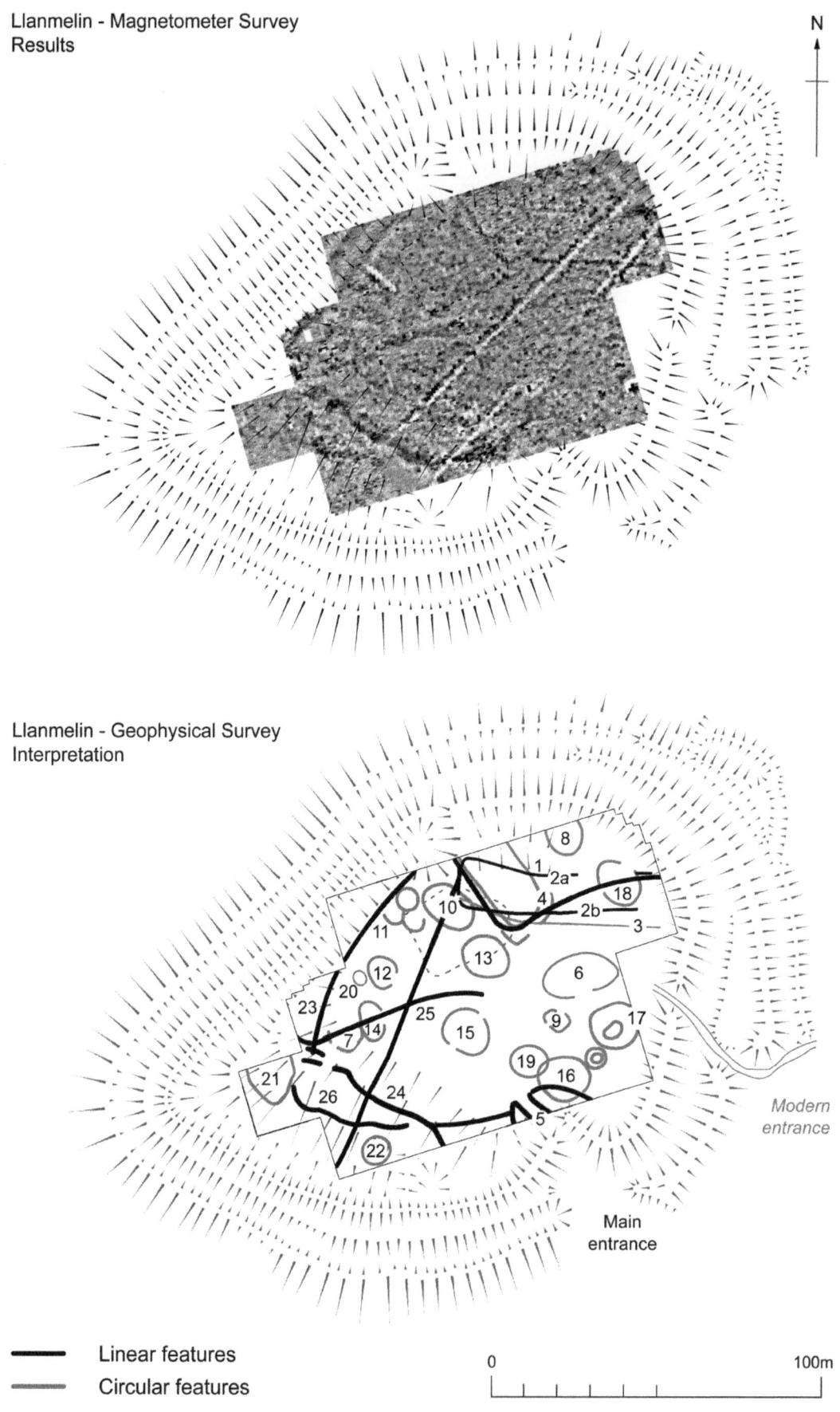

FIGURE 38. LLANMELIN. MAGNETOMETER SURVEY (TOP) AND INTERPRETATION OF GEOPHYSICAL SURVEY RESULTS (BOTTOM)

additional support by the presence of a straight length of faced stonework sealed under the eastern in-turn of the entrance earthwork directly opposite the pit (ibid., 279).

A further curved anomaly is situated several metres to the south-west of the western terminal and is seemingly related.

Feature 25 is a substantial linear anomaly, 2m+ wide and 55m long, which runs from just north of the gap between Features 23 and 24 towards the centre of the camp, before turning towards the entrance and fading out. It may mark a hollow-way running from a former western entrance into the interior of the hillfort.

Feature 26 is a substantial linear anomaly c.25m long, which runs along the bottom of Feature J. Given its size and format it probably marks a large length of ditch, possibly forming an outwork to an original western entrance.

Discussion
with Joshua Pollard

Llanmelin hillfort is likely to have had a long and complicated history with numerous major and minor episodes of re-modelling. The material culture excavated during the 1930s excavation suggests occupation, continuous or intermittent, took place from at least the 3rd century BC into the 1st century AD. The programme of topographic and geophysical survey described here has been extremely successful in providing additional structural detail to that recovered during the 1930s excavations. Taken together, a tentative sequence of construction and occupation can be outlined, though this will obviously need to be tested at some future date through targeted excavation:

Phase 1. The sequence could begin with one or more smaller, sub-rectangular, enclosures represented by earthworks D and E and geophysical anomalies 1, 2, 3 and 4 in the north-eastern part of the site. These are of a relatively insubstantial nature, more in line with 'farmstead'-size enclosures than a conventional hillfort.

Phase 2. This phase sees a massive re-modelling of the site, with the creation of a substantial univallate enclosure c.140 x 120m across, with a timber-laced rampart and entrances at the west and south. The western entrance may have been provided with an outwork (described by Feature 26), while that at the south was perhaps of simple construction. There is the possibility of a third entrance to the south-east, which was subsequently blocked then redefined by the line of the modern path.

Phase 3. The hillfort was extended to the west, and the western entrance not retained. The southern entrance was re-modelled to form an in-turned arrangement. Additional circuits of bank and ditch were added, creating a 'classic' multivallate hillfort; the banks being of simple dump or *glacis* construction. Putative roundhouses and compounds are indicated by the geophysical survey of the interior, and could belong to occupation throughout phases 1-3. Extra-mural occupation is suggested by the discovery of occupation deposits in the area later occupied by the Annexe (Nash-Williams 1933, 262-4).

Phase 4. At some point during the late Iron Age the rectilinear enclosures forming the Annexe were constructed to the south-east of the main entrance. The southern-most component of the Annexe may have been further sub-divided at a later date.

Phase 5. Limited Medieval occupation in the area of the Annexe.

Bibliography

Alcock, L. 1963. *Dinas Powys: an Iron Age, Dark Age and Early Medieval settlement site*. Cardiff: University of Wales Press

Alcock, L. 1987. *Economy, Society and Warfare among the Britons and Saxons*. Cardiff: University of Wales Press

Allen, J.R.L. 1998. Late Iron Age and Earliest Roman Calcite-tempered Ware from Sites on the Severn Estuary Levels: Character and Distribution. *Studia Celtica* 32, 27-41

Arnold, C. & Davies, J. 2000. *Roman and Early Medieval Wales*. Stroud: Alan Sutton

Babbidge, A. 1977. Reconnaissance excavations at Coed y Bwnydd, Bettws Newydd, 1969-1971. *Monmouthshire Antiquary* 3(3 & 4), 159-78

Barrett, J.C., Freeman, P.W.M. & Woodward, A. 2000. *Cadbury Castle, Somerset: the later prehistoric and early historic archaeology*. London: English Heritage, Archaeological Report 20

Bell, M. 1996. Environment in the First Millennium BC. In T.C. Champion & J.R. Collis (eds), *The Iron Age in Britain and Ireland: recent trends*, 5-16. Sheffield: J.R. Collis Publications/Department of Archaeology and Prehistory, University of Sheffield

Bell, M., Caseldine, A. & Neumann, H. 2000. *Prehistoric intertidal archaeology in the Welsh Severn estuary*. York: Council for British Archaeology, Research Report 120

Boon, G.C. 1987. *Isca: the legionary fortress of Caerleon*. Cardiff: National Museum of Wales

Bowden, M. & McOmish, D. 1987. The required barrier. *Scottish Archaeological Review* 4, 97-84

Boyd, W.E. 1988. Methodological problems in the analysis of fossil non-artifactual wood assemblages from archaeological sites. *Journal of Archaeological Science* 15, 603-19

Brewer, R.J. 2004. The Romans in Gwent. In M. Aldhouse-Green & R. Howell (eds), *Gwent County History. Volume 1, Gwent in prehistory and early history*, 205-43. Cardiff: University of Wales Press

Britnell, W. 1989. The Collfryn hillslope enclosure, Llansantffraid Deuddwr, Powys: excavations 1980-1982. *Proceedings of the Prehistoric Society* 55, 89-134

Buckland, P.C., Parker Pearson, M., Wigley, A. & Girling, M.A. 2001. Is there anybody out there? A reconsideration of the environmental evidence from the Breiddin hillfort, Powys, Wales. *Antiquaries Journal* 81, 51-76

Bersu, G. 1940. Excavations at Little Woodbury, Wiltshire, part 1. *Proceedings of the Prehistoric Society* 6, 30-111

Campbell, E. & Lane, A. 1993. Excavations at Longbury Bank, Dyfed, an Early Medieval Settlement in South Wales. *Medieval Archaeology* 37, 15-77

Chadwick, A.M. 1999. Digging ditches, but missing riches? Ways into the Iron Age and Romano-British cropmark landscapes of the north midlands. In B. Bevan (ed.), *Northern Exposure. Interpretative Devolution in the Iron Ages in Britain*, 149-71. Leicester: Leicester Archaeological Monographs

Children, G. & Nash, G. 1996. *Prehistoric Sites of Monmouthshire*. Woonton Almeley: Logaston Press

Clark, A. 1996. *Seeing Beneath the Soil: prospecting methods in archaeology*. London: Routledge

Clarke, S. 1999. Portskewett, new school development. *Archaeology in Wales* 39, 84-6

Collis, J. 1981. A theoretical study of hillforts. In G. Guilbert (ed.), *Hill-Fort Studies: essays for A.H.A Hogg*, 66-76. Leicester: Leicester University Press

Collis, J. 1996. Hill-forts, enclosures and boundaries. In T.C. Champion & J.R. Collis (eds), *The Iron Age in Britain and Ireland: recent trends*, 87-94. Sheffield: J.R. Collis Publications/Department of Archaeology and Prehistory, University of Sheffield

Coxe, W. 1801. *An Historical Tour of Monmouthshire*. London: Cadell and Davies

Crew, P. 1996. *Bloom refining and smithing, slags and other residues*. Historical Metallurgy Datasheet No. 6

Crummy, P. 2002. A preliminary account of the doctor's grave at Stanway, Colchester, England. In P.A. Baker & G. Carr (eds), *Practitioners, Practices and Patients: new approaches to medical archaeology and anthropology*, 47-57. Oxford: Oxbow Books

Cunliffe, B. 1984. Iron Age Wessex: continuity and change. In B. Cunliffe & D. Miles (eds), *Aspects of the Iron Age in Central Southern Britain*, 12-45. University of Oxford Committee for Archaeology

Cunliffe, B. 2005. *Iron Age Communities in Britain*. 4th edition. London: Routledge

Cunliffe, B. & Poole, C. 1991. *Danebury an Iron Age hillfort in Hampshire. Volume 5. The excavations, 1979-88: the finds*. London: Council for British Archaeology, Research Report 73

Dark, K.R. 1994. *Discovery by Design: the identification of secular elite settlements in western Britain AD400-700*. Oxford: British Archaeological Reports, British Series 237

Davies, J. 1967a. Excavations at Cae Summerhouse, Tythegston, Glam.: Second Interim Report. *Morgannwg* 11, 75-8

Davies, J. 1967b. Excavations at Caer Dynnaf, Llanblethian, Glam. 1965-1967. *Morgannwg* 11, 75-7

Dimblebly, G. 1978. *Plants and Archaeology.* London: Paladin

Dyer, J. 1976. Ravensburgh Castle, Hertfordshire. In D.W.Harding (ed.), *Hillforts: Later prehistoric earthworks in Britain and Ireland,* 153-9. London: Academic Press

Edwards, N. & Lane, A. (eds.) 1988. *Early Medieval Settlements in Wales AD 400-1100.* Bangor/Cardiff: University College of North Wales/University College, Cardiff

Ellison, A. & Drewett, P. 1971. Pits and post-holes in the British Early Iron Age: some alternative explanations. *Proceedings of the Prehistoric Society* 37(1), 183-94

Evans, A. & Metcalf, V. 1992. *Roman Gates Caerleon.* Oxford: Oxbow Books, monograph 15

Evans, E. & Maynard, D.J. 1997. Caerleon Lodge Hill cemetery: the Abbeyfield site 1992. *Britannia* 28, 169-243

Fitzpatrick, A.P. 1994. Outside in: the structure of an Early Iron Age house at Dunston Park, Thatcham, Berkshire. In A.P. Fitzpatrick & E.L. Morris (eds), *The Iron Age in Wessex: recent work,* 68-72. Salisbury: Trust for Wessex Archaeology

Gardner, W. & Savory, H.N. 1964. *Dinorben: a hill-fort occupied in Early Iron Age and Roman times.* Cardiff: National Museum of Wales

Geological Survey 1981. *Chepstow, 1:50,000.* (Solid & Drift, Sheet 250). Southampton: Ordnance Survey

Gilchrist, R., 1988. A Reappraisal of Dinas Powys: local exchange and specialised livestock production in 5th to 7th century Wales. *Medieval Archaeology* 32, 50-62

Giles, M. & Parker Pearson, M. 1999. Learning to Live in the Iron Age: dwelling and praxis. In B. Bevan (ed.), *Northern Exposure: interpretive devolution and the Iron Ages in Britain,* 217-31. Leicester: School of Archaeological Studies

Halstead, P. & O'Shea, J. 1982. A friend in need is a friend indeed: social storage and the origins of social ranking. In C. Renfrew & S. Shennan (eds), *Ranking, Resource and Exchange,* 92-9. Cambridge: Cambridge University Press

Haselgrove, C. 1992. Warfare, ritual and society in Iron Age Wessex. *Archaeological Journal* 149, 407-15

Haselgrove, C. 1997. Iron Age brooch deposition and chronology. In A. Gwilt & C. Haselgrove (eds), *Reconstructing Iron Age Societies,* 51-72. Oxford: Oxbow Books

Hill, J.D. 1995. *Ritual and Rubbish in the Iron Age of Wessex.* Oxford: British Archaeological Reports, British Series 242

Hill, J.D. 1996. Hill-forts and the Iron Age of Wessex. In T.C. Champion & J.R. Collis (eds), *The Iron Age in Britain and Ireland: recent trends,* 95-116. Sheffield: J.R. Collis Publications/Department of Archaeology and Prehistory, University of Sheffield

Hingley, R. 1990. Boundaries surrounding Iron Age and Romano-British settlements. *Scottish Archaeological Review* 7, 96-103

Hingley, R. 1997. Iron, ironworking and regeneration: a study of the symbolic meaning of metalworking in Iron Age Britain. In A. Gwilt & C. Haselgrove (eds), *Reconstructing Iron Age Societies,* 9-18. Oxford: Oxbow Books

Hodson, F.R. 1971. Three Iron Age brooches from Hammersmith. *British Museum Quarterly* 35, 50-57

Howell, R. 2000. The Demolition of the Roman Tetrapylon in Caerleon: an Erasure of Memory? *Oxford Journal of Archaeology* 19(4), 387-95

Howell, R. & Pollard, J. 2004. The Iron Age: settlement and material culture. In M. Aldhouse-Green & R. Howell (eds), *Gwent County History. Volume 1, Gwent in prehistory and early history,* 140-59. Cardiff: University of Wales Press

Hughes, G. 1996. *The Excavation of a Late Prehistoric and Romano-British Settlement at Thornwell Farm, Chepstow, Gwent, 1992.* Oxford: British Archaeological Reports, British Series 244

Hull, M.R. & Hawkes, C.F.C. 1987. *Corpus of ancient brooches in Britain by the late Mark Reginald Hull. Pre-Roman bow brooches.* Oxford: British Archaeological Reports, British Series 168

Ilic, J. 1991. *CSIRO Atlas of Hardwoods.* Bathurst, NSW: Crawford House Press

Jarrett, M.G. & Wrathmell, S. 1981. *Whitton: an Iron Age and Roman farmstead in South Glamorgan.* Cardiff: University of Wales Press

Jones, M. 1996. Plant exploitation. In T.C. Champion & J.R. Collis (eds), *The Iron Age in Britain and Ireland: recent trends,* 29-40. Sheffield: J.R. Collis Publications/Department of Archaeology and Prehistory, University of Sheffield

Leslie, J. 1962. The Camp, Tir y Mynach. *Archaeology in Wales* 2, 5-7

Lynch, F., Aldhouse-Green, S. & Davies, J.L. 2000. *Prehistoric Wales.* Stroud: Sutton Publishing

Manning, W.H. 1985. *Catalogue of the Romano-British iron tools, fittings and weapons in the British Museum.* London: British Museum Publications

Manning, W.H. 1993. *Report on the Excavations at Usk, 1965-1976: The Roman Pottery.* Cardiff: University of Wales Press

Manning, W.H. 2001. *Roman Wales.* Cardiff: University of Wales Press

Manning, W.H. 2004. The Romans: conquest and after. In M. Aldhouse-Green & R. Howell (eds),

Gwent County History. Volume 1, Gwent in prehistory and early history, 178-204. Cardiff: University of Wales Press

Morris, E.L. 1982. Iron Age pottery from western Britain: another petrological study. In I. Freestone, C. Johns & T. Potter (eds), *Current Research in Ceramics: thin-section studies*, 15-28. London: British Museum, Occasional Paper 32

Morris, E.L. 1983. *Salt and Pottery Distribution in Western Britain during the 1st Millennium BC*. Unpublished PhD thesis, University of Southampton

Morris, E.L. 1985. Prehistoric salt distributions: two case studies from western Britain. *Bulletin of the Board of Celtic Studies* 32, 336-79

Morris, E.L. 1994. Production and distribution of pottery and salt in Iron Age Britain: a review. *Proceedings of the Prehistoric Society* 60, 371-93

Morris, E.L. 1997. Where is the Danebury ware? In A. Gwilt & C. Haselgrove (eds), *Reconstructing Iron Age Societies*, 36-9. Oxford: Oxbow Books

Morris, E.L. 2001. Briquetage and salt production and distribution systems: a comparative study. In T. Lane & E.L. Morris (eds), *A Millennium of Saltmaking: prehistoric and Romano-British salt production in the Fenland*, 389-404. Heckington: Heritage Trust of Lincolnshire/Fenland Management Project

Musson, C.R. 1991. *The Breiddin Hillfort: a later prehistoric settlement in the Welsh Marches*. London: Council for British Archaeology, Research Report 76

Nash-Williams, V. 1933. An early Iron Age hillfort at Llanmelin, near Caerwent, Monmouthshire', *Archaeologia Cambrensis* 88, 1933, 237-315.

Nash-Williams, V. 1939. An early Iron Age coastal camp at Sudbrook. *Archaeologia Cambrensis* 94, 42-79

Nayling, N. & Caseldine, A. 1997. *Excavations at Caldicot, Gwent: Bronze Age Palaeochannels in the Lower Nedern Valley*. London: CBA, Research Report 108

Olding, F. 2000. *The Prehistoric Landscapes of the Eastern Black Mountains*. Oxford: British Archaeological Reports, British Series 297

Oswald, A. 1997. A doorway on the past: practical and mystic concerns in the orientation of roundhouse doorways. In A. Gwilt & C. Haselgrove (eds), *Reconstructing Iron Age Societies*, 87-95. Oxford: Oxbow Books

Parker Pearson, M. 1996. Food, fertility and front doors in the first millennium BC. In T.C. Champion & J.R. Collis (eds), *The Iron Age in Britain and Ireland: recent trends*, 117-132. Sheffield: J.R. Collis Publications/Department of Archaeology and Prehistory, University of Sheffield

Peacock, D.P.S. 1968. A petrological study of certain Iron Age pottery from western England. *Proceedings of the Prehistoric Society* 34, 414-27

Peacock, D.P.S. 1977. Ceramics in Roman and medieval archaeology. In D.P.S. Peacock (ed), *Pottery in early commerce*, 21-34. London: Academic Press

Piggott, S. 1962. *The West Kennet Long Barrow: excavations 1955-56*. London: HMSO

Probert, L.A. 1976. Twyn-y-Gaer hill-fort, Gwent: an interim assessment. In G.C. Boon & J.M. Lewis (eds), *Welsh Antiquity*, 105-19. Cardiff: National Museum of Wales

Rackham, O. 1977. Neolithic woodland management in the Somerset Levels: Garvin's, Walton Heath and Rowland's tracks. *Somerset Levels Papers* 3, 65-71

RCAHMW 1976. *Glamorgan Vol. 1, Part 2: the Iron Age and Roman Occupation* London: HMSO

Savory, H.N. 1971. *Excavations at Dinorben, 1965-9*. Cardiff: National Museum of Wales

Savory, H.N. 1976. Welsh hillforts: a reappraisal of recent research. In D.W. Harding (ed.), *Hillforts: later prehistoric earthworks in Britain and Ireland*. London: Academic Press

Schweingruber, F.H. 1978. *Microscopic Wood Anatomy*. Teufen: F. Fluck-Wirth

Sell, S.H. 2001. Recent excavation and survey work at Sudbrook Camp, Portskewett, Monmouthshire (ST 507873). *Studia Celtica* 35, 109-41

Sharples, N. 1991a. *Maiden Castle: excavations and field survey 1985-6*. London: English Heritage

Sharples, N. 1991b. Warfare in the Iron Age of Wessex. *Scottish Archaeological Review* 8, 79-89

Spencer, B. 1983. Limestone-tempered pottery from South Wales in the Late Iron Age and Early Roman period. *Bulletin of the Board of Celtic Studies* 30, 405-19

Stead, I.M. 1979. *The Arras culture*. York: Yorkshire Philosophical Society

Stead, I.M. 1991. *Iron Age cemeteries in East Yorkshire: Excavations at Burton Fleming, Rudston, Garton-on-the-Wolds, and Kirkburn*. London: English Heritage Archaeological Report 22

Stead, I.M. & Rigby, V. 1989. *Verulamium: the King Harry Lane Site*. London: English Heritage

Thompson, J. 1994. Wood charcoals from Tropical sites: a contribution to methodology and interpretation. In J.G. Hather (ed.), *Tropical Archaeobotany: Applications and new developments*, 9-33. London: Routledge

Trueman, D. 1988. *Hill-forts and the Iron Age in Gwent*. Newport: Newport Museum and Art Gallery

Wainwright, G.J. 1967. *Coygan Camp, a prehistoric, Romano-British and dark age settlement in Carmarthenshire*. Cardiff: Cambrian Archaeological Association

Wainwright, G.J. & Davies, S.M. 1995. *Balksbury Camp Hampshire. Excavations 1973 and 1981*. London: English Heritage Archaeological Report 4

Welch, F.B.A. & Trotter, F.M. 1961. *Geology of the Country around Monmouth and Chepstow. Explanation of Sheets 233 and 250*. Memoirs of the Geological Survey of Great Britain. London: HMSO

Wells, P.S. 2001. *Beyond Celts, Germans and Scythians*. London: Duckworth

Whittle, A.W.R. 1989. Two later Bronze Age occupations and an Iron Age channel on the Gwent foreshore. *Bulletin of the Board of Celtic Studies* 36, 200-23

Whittle, E. 1992. *A Guide to Ancient and Historic Wales*: Glamorgan and Gwent. London: HMSO

Williams, A. 1939. Prehistoric and Roman Pottery in the Museum of the Royal Institution of South Wales, Swansea. *Archaeologia Cambrensis* 94, 21-9

Williams, A. 1940. The Excavation of Bishopston Valley Promontory Fort, Glamorgan. *Archaeologia Cambrensis* 95, 9-19

Williams, A. 1941. The Excavation of High Penard Promontory Fort, Glamorgan. *Archaeologia Cambrensis* 96, 23-30

Woodward, A. 1996. The prehistoric and native pottery. In G. Hughes, *The Excavation of a Late Prehistoric and Romano-British Settlement at Thornwell Farm, Chepstow, Gwent*, 1992, 36-45. Oxford: British Archaeological Reports, British Series 244

Zienkiewicz, D. 1986. *The Legionary Fortress Baths at Caerleon*. Cardiff: Cadw/National Museum of Wales

www.ingramcontent.com/pod-product-compliance
Lightning Source LLC
Chambersburg PA
CBHW061549010526
44115CB00023B/2993